MW00423999

ON NATIONALISM

ON NATIONALISM

ROMILA THAPAR
A. G. NOORANI
SADANAND MENON

ALEPH

ALEPH

ALEPH BOOK COMPANY
An independent publishing firm
promoted by *Rupa Publications India*

First published in India in 2016
by Aleph Book Company
7/16 Ansari Road, Daryaganj
New Delhi 110 002

ISBN: 978-93-83064-11-3

5 7 9 10 8 6

Printed at Saurabh Printers Pvt. Ltd, Noida

CONTENTS

FOREWORD

We live in troubled and troubling times. Not a day passes without some fresh outrage being reported in the media or being talked about in our neighbourhoods. None of this is new. We live, as we have for the last couple of centuries now, in a country that is poor, violent, corrupt, overpopulated, misogynistic, unequal, and prone to sectarian violence, terrorism and environmental disasters, to name just a few of the challenges we have to cope with, and it is unrealistic not to expect bad things to occur. We all hope such tragedies will be eliminated, that we will touch greatness, but unless all those who are able to make this happen actually rise above their own selfish agendas and begin to work in concert and with tremendous dedication, it would be safe to say that for the majority there will be no radical change for the better any time soon, despite the fact that some of our countrymen work hard to make a difference. What we do have, imperfect though they may be, are freedom of expression, liberalism in some pockets, inclusiveness, cultural vibrancy, the right to practise whatever faith we choose without let or hindrance and so on—the fundamental rights bequeathed to us by our founding fathers. In recent times, though, a very vocal set of politicians, sectarian organizations, godmen, trolls and assorted thugs have begun to brazenly attack some of the values that invest this country. Never before have they been assailed with such impunity.

One of the most contested ideas in twenty-first-century India is nationalism. It is easy to see why. If the forces I am speaking of (usually right wing and majoritarian) succeed in recasting nationalism in a straitjacket that suits their own narrow ends, they will, they hope, usher in a thousand-year rule of the theocratic kind. That they will probably not succeed in their aims, given the multifariousness of their 'co-religionists' and the tens of millions of 'minorities' (by this I mean not only religious minorities, but everyone who has a problem with religious fundamentalism and the notion of living in a violent theocracy—else, why is every sane, secular person opposed to the likes of ISIS or Boko Haram?) who might not take kindly to becoming second-class citizens is small consolation because considerable damage will have been done to Indian society by then. We need to constantly remind ourselves that the only way for India to survive and thrive is to continue to be the open, inclusive country that our founding fathers fought to bring into being, and that all of us inherited at birth. That is why this book is being published—to make its own small contribution to the ongoing debate. It seeks to provide interested readers with a range of thoughtful opinions on why it is important to understand what nationalism is, and why certain kinds of nationalism may be seen as true and others false.

◆

It could be said that nationalism is subtly threaded into our DNA; it doesn't intrude upon our daily lives but makes itself manifest on demand, often when it is under threat in some way. Some years ago, my wife, Rachna, and I had occasion to think about our nationality, and the nationalism it engendered. We had just become eligible for citizenship of the country we then lived in. Our home was in a city that routinely featured in lists of the most congenial places in the world to live and work in. We had a very brief discussion about whether we wanted to adopt a new nationality. Despite the fact that the country we lived in offered some enormous advantages over our own, there was no doubt in our minds that changing our nationality wasn't an option. We were born Indian and would die Indian. Some of Rachna's reasons paralleled mine. For both of us, our decisions were based on what could be called a mix of nationalism and patriotism. George Orwell, the British writer and humanist, has an interesting way of differentiating between the two. He wrote in an essay entitled 'Notes on Nationalism', published in 1945: 'Nationalism is not to be confused with patriotism. Both words are normally used in so vague a way that any definition is liable to be challenged, but one must draw a distinction between them, since two different and even opposing ideas are involved. By "patriotism" I mean devotion to a particular place and a particular way of life, which one believes to be the best in the world but has no wish to force on other people... Nationalism, on the other hand, is inseparable from the desire for power. The abiding purpose of every nationalist is to secure more power and prestige, *not* for himself but for the nation or other unit in which he has chosen to sink his individuality.' Others have defined nationalism a little differently but basically it was why we decided to stick with the passport with the gilt-embossed Ashoka Chakra.

As I was writing this foreword, I was reminded of the things that went through my mind that wintry evening almost a decade ago. In sum, my decision was based on a sense of belonging to a larger community, both real and imagined, that I had inherited when I was born. This community had nothing to do with caste, creed, region, language, but rather all of these and more. It had to do with memories of my grandmother's sari, the softest garment I had ever touched (the softness of her sari was because my maternal grandparents led a middle-class life in small-town India with no frills. My grandmother only possessed a few cotton saris that had been washed often; this lent the material an extraordinary delicacy); the feeling of joy when, as students, we received news of the defeat of Indira Gandhi after the dark days of the Emergency; the sadness that enveloped us when we heard of the demolition of the Babri Masjid; the exhilaration we felt when M. S. Dhoni hit the winning six to seal India's victory in the World Cup; the great sense of satisfaction I felt when I read and published

Vikram Seth's *A Suitable Boy* or P. Sainath's wrenching stories about India's poorest districts; the awe I felt when I first glimpsed the most beautiful lake in the world, the Pangong Tso, in Ladakh. Underpinning all this was, of course, the decades of learning and doing, the friends, the family, the shared history and heritage. As with the good stuff so with the bad. The anger I felt over all the things that bothered me was keener when they had to do with India than any other place on earth. No other country could provide that feeling of belonging. That was my nationalism; it was the sense that I was an integral part of something much larger than myself which no one could take away from me, not now or ever. It was a concept, it was a tangible reality, and in its most abstract form it included every Indian, known and unknown, in the best possible way.

It is this nationalism that is under siege today. It is this nationalism that certain extremely motivated people are seeking to make exclusionary and cast in a mould of their own discriminatory making that will segregate us all into superior Indians or second-class Indians, those who belong and those who don't. These elements are seeking to subvert the rights guaranteed to every citizen under the Constitution and are attempting to redefine the very essence of India. If they succeed in their efforts, they will destroy the country we love, the only India we have ever known.

On Nationalism goes deep into the concept and practice of nationalism (or patriotism), whether historical, legal or cultural. One of our most important public intellectuals, Romila Thapar, differentiates between nationalism and pseudo-nationalism, among other things, in the lead essay. The brilliant lawyer and writer A. G. Noorani points out the dangers of using the law of sedition indiscriminately against writers, artists, students and political opponents. And the senior journalist and cultural commentator Sadanand Menon writes about the perils of destroying the nation's vibrant culture by forcing it to conform to theological and other imperatives.

Today, some of the important questions we need to ask ourselves are as follows: 1) What sort of India do we want? 2) What sort of Indians do we want to be? and 3) What sort of country are we going to leave behind for future generations? Nearly eighty years ago, during an intervention in the Bombay legislature, Dr B. R. Ambedkar made a statement that answers these questions. He said: '…I do not believe there is any place in this country for any particular culture, whether it is a Hindu culture, or a Muhammadan culture or a Kanarese culture or a Gujarati culture. There are things we cannot deny, but they are not to be cultivated as advantages, they are to be treated as disadvantages, as something which divides our loyalty and takes away from us our common goal. That common goal is the building up of the feeling that we are all Indians. I do not like what some people say, that we are Indians first and Hindus afterwards or Muslims afterwards. I am not satisfied with that… I do not want that our loyalty as Indians should be in the slightest way affected by any competitive loyalty whether that loyalty arises out of our religion, out of our culture or out of our language. I want all people to be Indians first, Indians last and nothing else but Indians…'

These are words that are as relevant today as in 1938 when they were first spoken. We ignore them at our peril.

D. D.
New Delhi
29 May 2016

REFLECTIONS
ON
NATIONALISM
AND
HISTORY

ROMILA THAPAR

For Indians of my age who grew up on the cusp of Independence, nationalism was in the air we breathed. Nationalism was not something problematic. It was an identity with the nation and its society. The identity and consciousness of being Indian did not initially need to be defined. We understood nationalism to be Indian nationalism and not Hindu or Muslim or any other kind of religious or other nationalism, and a clear distinction was made between nationalism and other loyalties. Nationalism could only be Indian. And Indian meant that which was above all the smaller loyalties to religion, caste, ethnicity and region. Nationalism meant differentiating between the nation and the state, and it was clear that no government could take upon itself the rights of a nation. Sovereignty resides with the nation and not with the government. A nation referred to the people that inhabited a territory who saw themselves as an evolved community created by drawing upon the range of communities that existed prior to the nation. It was based on a shared history, interests and aspirations frequently expressed in a common culture that in turn drew from multiple cultures.

At the most visible level, a nation is identified with territory. For the Indian this was the territory of British India that the colony hoped to inherit on becoming a nation. This had to be bifurcated with Partition in 1947, and that was problematic when identified with the erstwhile territory of British India. So the territory of what constituted India had to be redefined.

Nevertheless, the subcontinent remained the framework when thinking about India in historical terms. We learnt from history that through the centuries there was a constant changing of boundaries and the coexistence of many political units within the subcontinent. This raised the question of whether a permanent boundary of a nation state was feasible, but for the purposes of nationalism it was assumed to be as permanent as possible, with the caveat that it could change.

This also turned our attention to the real entity of nationalism and that was the people who inhabited the territory. This was meant literally and it included all the people, irrespective of their sub-identities of religion, caste, language, region and such like. There was an axiomatic belief that the primary concern of nationalism was to ensure the welfare of the entire society, and of all its citizens. This was defined as establishing the equality of all citizens and their entitlement to human rights. National interest meant ensuring that every citizen lived with dignity. This required both economic growth and social justice as fundamental to the establishing of a nation. These essentials of a nation were discussed extensively, especially in universities and research centres, in the first couple of decades after Independence.

◆

Nationalism had, and has, much to do with understanding one's society and finding one's identity as a member of that society. It cannot be reduced merely to waving flags and shouting slogans and penalizing people for not shouting slogans like 'Bharat Mata ki Jai'. This smacks of a lack of confidence among those making the demand for slogans. Nationalism requires a far greater commitment to attending to the needs of the nation rather than sloganeering, and that too with slogans focusing on territory or ones that have a limited acceptability. As was recently said, it is indeed ironic that an Indian who refuses to shout this slogan is immediately declared as anti-national, but an Indian who has deliberately not paid his taxes or stashed away black money is not declared as such.

The question of what is national and what is anti-national does depend on what is understood by nationalism. A commitment to the nation if it encourages concern for and an ethical attitude towards other citizens of the same nation is always commended. However this should not be expressed by vicious hostility towards neighbouring nations as also happens. Hostility, in particular situations, has to be tempered with reason and this is one difference between good governance and bad. Nationalism, therefore, cannot be without its limits and the limits have to be carefully worked out.

The question is sometimes asked whether there was nationalism in pre-modern times. Historians would think not. Internal distinctions are part of the stratification of every society. Yet, as an entity, a society differentiates itself from others. Societies in the past were more often known by the characteristics of their elite. An example of this is the defining of civilizations. Indian civilization was located in the territory of British India, its language was said to be Sanskrit and its religion Hindu. This definition was of course the contribution of colonial scholarship that we have dutifully appropriated, without giving attention to other significant features that went into the making of the civilization, or questioning whether this was all that was required for defining a civilization. The culture of the dominant elite went into defining civilization. Non-elites and their cultural patterns, especially in rural areas, were hardly recognized. They had a circumscribed existence. Even within this very limited definition of civilization, physical boundaries constantly changed, languages changed, religions mutated, as did the cultural identity and what was recorded as history. These again pertained more to the elites than to others.

Nationalism as it evolved historically was inclusive and drew on the idea of the unification of diverse groups to form a new community of citizens. Nevertheless, there were, and are, some ideologies that claim to be nationalisms but where the identity gives priority to only one group, and this acts as a force of divisiveness. This has led to identifying genuine nationalism as a form of unification. It does not require the cultural idiom of a specific community and often creates new idioms. More correctly, therefore, concepts of nations based on a single exclusive identity—religious, linguistic, ethnic and similar single identities—are actually pseudo-nationalisms and should be precluded from being called a nationalism, without the accompanying qualifier of their identity.

Thus, in India, we distinguish between secular, anti-colonial nationalism that was the mainstay of the national freedom movement, and the other movements that called themselves nationalisms but were doubtful as such and were more correctly religious or communal nationalisms that drew their identity from individual religions, such as the Muslim, Hindu and Sikh nationalisms. Many historians would refrain from calling these nationalisms. The rise of such categories can, if one chooses to be charitable, be called sub-nationalisms, although some may hesitate to use any association with nationalism for such groups.

Historians see the nation as a modern concept and do not trace it to antiquity. It emerges at a specific point of time that dates to the post-Enlightenment period in Europe. It coincides with a major change, namely the emergence of societies out of the earlier feudal or similar systems into what became the interrelation of industrialization with the growth of capitalism and an economy based on both capitalism and colonialism. As a universalizing concept it lent itself to asserting political power and that became the direction taken by most nationalisms.

The nation is different from the state and from government. The state can have different forms of government as it did in the pre-modern past. The use of the term 'nation state' qualifies the kind of state. Nationalism is a function of the nation. Conceptually, it consolidates aspects of the nation such as democracy, territory and power and endorses the value systems that ensure equal rights and justice. The nation is generally not centrally and directly ruled by a dynasty, it is the representatives of the people who govern it in a democratic system. In other words, ultimately, it is the people who determine the nation. Unfortunately, this definition is not appreciated by the many who think nationalism is only about shouting slogans and keeping the territory unchanged. The question of nationalism and anti-nationalism when it hovers over territory is not as central when compared to the other aspects of a nation that all its citizens share, even if territory does on occasion become the focus.

A few decades ago, there was much discussion on what goes into the making of nationalism. The discussion was varied since nationalism is not a tangible object but an abstract concept. Benedict Anderson, the political scientist and historian, referred in his influential book *Imagined Communities: Reflections on the Origin and Spread of Nationalism* to an imagined community as constructed by people who think of themselves as a community with common perceptions that unite them. The unity was more feasible in modern times than in earlier periods because of the spread of literacy with the assistance of the printing press and the reading of newspapers, etc. To this one could add, if so desired, the influence of television and the cinema as sustaining or even assisting in creating a national feeling.

In *Nations and Nationalism* (1983), Ernest Gellner, the British social anthropologist and a leading thinker on the subject of nationalism, linked it more closely to a new kind of society that grew out of an earlier society and differed from it in various ways. It permitted the growth of an impersonal society where individuals were bonded through defining a shared culture and learning a shared history. Again, to this one could add that the observance of the same code of laws was also a binding factor.

Eric J. Hobsbawm, the British thinker and historian, made a connection in *Nations and Nationalism since 1780* (1990) between history and nationalism and explained how history is reconstructed in a way that suits the ideology of nationalism and is essential to the construction of nationalism. It is essential to the making of a state and this incorporates not just the elite but also the less privileged. Nationalism may begin with ideas among the elite but its propagation involves having mass support. Initially, anti-colonial Indian nationalism had a more limited role as compared to what it became when it was converted into a mass movement in the twentieth century. History plays a crucial role in both creating the basis of the unity and for sustaining it. Hobsbawm compares the role of history to nationalism with that of the poppy to the heroin addict.

This is one explanation for why history in India has become the arena of struggle between the secular nationalists and those endorsing varieties of religious or pseudo-nationalisms. Nationalist historical writing visualized history as supportive of the interlinking of the communities that constituted Indian society. Occasionally there were deviations from this when a particular religious community was given greater centrality than was appropriate to a nationalist perspective. Differences among historians arise when the pseudo-nationalisms exaggerate the importance of a single history of one religious community as being the pre-eminent history of the nation, and denigrate and distort the history of other communities. The public historical confrontations today are between secular historians and those who write history from the perspective of communal 'nationalisms'. Needless to say, the discipline of history has moved well beyond this debate, but the latter are oblivious of this since they are grounded in their political agenda.

We have seen this clearly in the nationalist history written by historians who were part of the anti-colonial nationalist movement with their emphasis on understanding Indian society in terms of its continuity and common characteristics. As a contrast to this is the 'history' as written by the RSS and Hindutva ideologues for whom the past has only to do with Hindu history of the early period and the victimization of Hindus under Muslim tyranny in the medieval period. They speak of Hindus being enslaved for a thousand years by Muslim rule, but do not pause for a moment to give thought to at least two facts.

One is that caste Hindus victimized the lower castes, Dalits and Adivasis for two thousand or more years, and most caste Hindus, with a few exceptions, regarded it as quite legitimate. Some continue to do so. Secondly, that some of the more powerful propagation of Hindu religious sects dates to the last thousand years—such as the Bhakti and Tantric traditions in northern India—and these characterize the kind of Hinduism that is practised by the larger number of people currently called Hindu in the census reports.

The bhajans of Mira and Surdas and the poetry of Kabir and Tukaram, as well as the many renderings of the Ramayana, such as by Tulasidasa and by Krittivasa, were all composed in this period. Their popularity was so immense among various communities of people that phrases and verses from these compositions became idioms in the languages of their composition such as Hindi, Bengali and Marathi. This experience was paralleled in other languages of the subcontinent.

Furthermore, some of the most notable achievements in knowledge of various kinds, from literature to mathematics, can be ascribed to Hindu scholars who were recognized as such during this period. Among these achievements were some singular traditions of Hindu culture as well as some highly creative interfacing with other religions and cultures. Far from being victimized, Hindu culture flourished along with other cultures in these centuries. This is demonstrated in texts such as Madhava's *Sarvadarshanasangraha* on the prevailing schools of philosophy and Samayasundara's *Artharatnavali* on linguistic explorations and belief systems. Sayana wrote his renowned exposition of the Rigveda in the fourteenth century. Commentaries on, and digests of, earlier social codes and the Dharmashastras reflected new situations. Some incorporated discussions on the status of those converted to Islam. Others debated the status of the now greatly empowered temple priests who were performers of rituals as well as administrators in the many wealthy temples that became a part of the urban scene.

Intensely devotional poetry was written by poets, some of whom were born Muslim but worshipped Hindu deities. One of the best known among them was Sayyad Ibrahim, popularly referred to as Raskhan, whose dohas and bhajans dedicated to the deity Krishna were widely recited in the sixteenth century and are still remembered by devotees of Krishna and others. The intermingling of cultures is also evident in the new kinds of classical music that was composed and sung at the courts of this period. Best known among these was the creation and evolution of Dhrupad, regarded by many as the finest form of Hindustani classical music. The Mughal court became the most impressive patron of the translation of many Sanskrit religious texts into

Persian. Among these the Mahabharata (translated as the *Razmnamah*) and the Bhagavad Gita hold pride of place. Brahmana priests worked together with Persian scholars on these translations encouraged by Hindu and Muslim noblemen at the courts.

This was also the period when the gurus, pirs and sants wandered from place to place, preached their understanding of religion, founded sects and sometimes settled somewhere that became a place of pilgrimage. They were people of every possible religious background and their teachings were often a religious melange that defied identification with a particular religion. Some were localized and others spread across the subcontinent, like the Nathapantha. They ranged from informal religious sects to well-established formal sects with large bodies of followers. Such sects crossed religious and social barriers without a thought and none could stop them because their followings were so large. When they became well established even royal patrons received them cordially. They were the opinion-makers of their times.

This does not support the idea of victimized Hindus but rather of people of different cultures investigating their cultures in order to find points of integration or of disagreement. Nor should this be taken as an indication of complete harmony among the various cultures. Since there were inequalities, there would have been points of dislocation and confrontation, as indeed are only too evident in the pre-Islamic history of India. But to speak of victimization is merely to try and impose a particular kind of image of the past onto our present perceptions so as to propagate communal hostility. The purpose of historical research is to try and understand the interface between the cultures of the past and explain the different kinds of relationships they may have had. But if history is subjected to fabrication in order to make it the excuse for aggression against another community in contemporary times, then we cannot expect it to provide an understanding and an explanation of what happened in the past and why.

Religious nationalism, or communalism as some prefer to call it, both Muslim and Hindu, was marginal to the anti-colonial movement. They did not confront the colonial power, focused as the two communalisms were on attacking each other in the interests of establishing an Islamic and a Hindu state. The catalyst in many anti-colonial nationalisms was the focus on removing the colonial power which was seen as exploiting the colony, accompanied by the colonized wanting the rights of representation in what was ideally seen as a democratic system still to be established. Both were essential to how the middle class saw its role and this was prior to its own eventual success that led it on occasion to curb these rights.

What we take to be nationalism can be a positive force if it calls for the unification of communities, but equally it can be a divisive and therefore negative force if it underlines exclusive rights for one community on the basis of a single identifying factor. We've seen a very severe example of negative nationalism in the case of Germany in the 1930s when the Nazis propagated the idea of the purity of the Aryan race and the origin of European Aryans. This was central to the Fascist understanding of European society and crucial to German Fascism and was not absent in Italian Fascism either.

The Aryans were said to be superior racially and culturally and were not only given priority of place in German society, but it was even argued that the purity of German society could be achieved by annihilating the non-Aryans. The non-Aryans were the Jews and the Gypsies and they were not merely excluded but were physically annihilated. This began with segregating and abusing them and ended with taking them forcibly, trainload by trainload, to special camps where they were gassed and killed. This was done through the Holocaust and the literal decimation of the Jewish population in Germany, using up-to-date scientific techniques. Liberal thinkers and intellectuals were special targets of attack and many among them had to flee Germany although many more were gassed in the concentration camps. The irony was that the Jews were so well integrated into German society that they were major contributors to German culture, science and intellectual life. Those that did manage to escape became catalysts in the enrichment of intellectual life in Europe and the USA in the post-World War II period. The loss was that of the Fascist countries. I am referring to this because these kinds of sentiments of excluding minorities is what we often hear in our own society and in other societies, with reference to people who are, for obnoxious reasons, regarded as unwanted.

However, where nationalism has been inclusive, the effect has tended to be positive, at least initially. For example, the kind of nationalism we seldom refer to but whose ideology is pertinent to the Indian situation—African nationalism—was based on the idea of what came to be called Negritude. This emerged as an ideology from the Caribbean countries in the 1930s and through contact with Africans in other places, and its immediate context was French colonialism. Aimé Césaire, Léopold Senghor and Léon Damas formulated the idea. This brought together an African consciousness that stretched from Africa to the Caribbean to North America. It was an inclusive nationalism of a very extraordinary kind and I think we would do well to study it some more.

The main thrust of Negritude was that it was an anti-colonial nationalism initially critiquing French colonialism as an example of European dominance. It celebrated the black African identity and brought together black critics of imperialism. The derogatory term, negre (black), to mean black people, was deliberately turned on its head and given a positive meaning of black identity. This in a sense also caused it to challenge and oppose the popular 'race science' of the time in Europe and the notion that Africans are primitive and savage. Negritude became a major literary and philosophical movement among black writers, many of whom wrote from a secular perspective. Although the reinterpretation of religion was a subject of interest, culture was not defined as religion but as the articulation at many levels of the groups that constituted black societies in these various countries. As a precursor to decolonization in Africa and the Caribbean, and because of its association with the anti-slavery movement in the USA, it became crucial to black nationalism.

In later years it, too, was critiqued when it was thought that the racial identity had become too singular in the definition. In areas where Negritude was influential, the population was not limited to Africans, especially in the Caribbean. Jean-Paul Sartre, the French philosopher who was appreciative of Negritude, referred to it as anti-racist racism. Later, some African writers were opposed to it because it accepted distinctive racial cultures and their characteristics. This was regarded as complicit with colonial thought. Other theories entered the discussion on Negritude, questioning whether it drew on biological or cultural roots in arguing for a difference. The point that I would like to make is that any term used in one historical context can be differently used in another. Therefore, the historical context is significant in discussing the term. Further, what goes by the name of nationalism can be used in various ways and it is necessary to seek out the historical context of each and for its political and cultural function in the society to which it refers.

But let me return to the Indian situation and the evolution of nationalist ideas in India. This was tied to colonialism. All of us in the Indian subcontinent, not to mention other ex-colonies, have faced the same questions of how to define ourselves as citizens of a new nation. This relates to the question of identity or identities. We in India thought the answer was simple—it was the single identity of being Indian. But the reality on the ground has turned it into a complex question without a simple answer because even a single identity can subsume others. The utopia that we had wished for has retreated in the face of identities in conflict.

History, as we were taught in school and even later, was a representation of the past based on information that we had gathered from the past. In the case of colonies such as India, colonial scholars claimed that they were writing the history of the colony since there was supposedly an absence of historical writing in the cultures of the colony. Therefore, a history had to be constructed for the region by colonial scholars and this they proceeded to do. But when this history was used to construct identities relevant only to the present but with claims of having roots in the past, it became necessary for historians to unpack the past to discover the actual roots. In this process of unpacking, one realizes that the past registers changes that could alter its representation. The past does not remain static.

In examining the construction of the past in the form in which we had inherited it from colonial scholarship, it was further seen that aspects of nationalist thinking had borrowed from this colonial legacy. The colonial reconstruction of the past in India was the poppy of which Hobsbawm speaks. Nationalism was built by coalescing many identities and aspiring to be inclusive of the entire society. It inevitably opposed the defining of the nation on the basis of a single identity projected as superior to the rest. For this claim to superiority, an imagined history is put forth endorsing the dominance of the supposedly superior group. Inclusiveness is undoubtedly problematic since every society since early times has overlooked the need for equality and has acquiesced in the dominance of some and the subordination of others. These frequently become the issues of conflict. Inequality is thus predictable and results in multiple identities competing for visibility. Yet the wish for an egalitarian society, or one relatively so, has been a feature in envisioning future utopias.

In our present post-colonial times in India, the multiple identities of the period contemporary with nationalism have surfaced and become visible. But the historical context is constantly changing. Each identity demands priority for itself and asks to be treated as exclusive, and this becomes an agency for mobilization. The inclusiveness of the earlier anti-colonial nationalism is set aside. In claiming legitimacy from the past, that past itself is converted into an assemblage of what is most desired in the present. Separating what might actually have happened from the fantasies of political ideologues masquerading as specialists in religion makes it necessary to understand historical knowledge.

◆

Among our current identities in India, the more prominent ones go back to colonial times and were usually constructed with links to pre-modern history. Examples of this are identities of race, language, caste, tribe and religion. Economic poverty and inequality is the colonial heritage of large segments of the population. In the couple of centuries just prior to colonization, India and China were leading economies.

This changed with the coming of colonialism. The identities constructed by colonialism in the nineteenth century became the prisms through which Europe viewed the past of India. The history of the colony was of prime concern to the colonial ruler in order to govern its strange peoples and to exploit its wealth and, to some extent, to understand its culture, so alien to European eyes.

Some of this concern resulted in path-breaking work on deciphering scripts, revealing tangible history through excavations, and investigating language through philology—analysing its linguistic components. Much effort was made to collect data through archaeological excavations, linguistic surveys, and a systematic programme of collecting texts. The oral traditions of bardic compositions were also part of this effort. Ancient scripts, such as Brahmi, were deciphered so that inscriptions could now be read, thereby providing extensive fresh information, not always in conformity with the normative and sacred texts, and therefore presenting an interesting alternative picture of society. All this data had to be organized and interpreted. The organization was efficient but the interpretation reinforced colonial theories. Nevertheless, as Lord Curzon, the viceroy of India from 1899 to 1905, stated, all this was 'the necessary furniture of Empire'.

Three arguments were foundational to the colonial interpretation of Indian history. The first was periodization. James Mill in *The History of British India* published 1817-1826, almost two hundred years ago, argued for three periods, labelled in accordance with the religion of the rulers: Hindu civilization, Muslim civilization and the British period. The divisions were endorsed by the assumption that the units of Indian society have always been monolithic religious communities—primarily the Hindu and the Muslim—which were mutually hostile. Religion was believed to have superseded all other authority.

On the basis of their numbers in the Census of 1872 and subsequently, the Hindus came to be called the majority community, and the Muslims and others were the minority communities. It was argued that there was an absence of historical change in India, therefore all institutions were static until the coming of the colonial power. The only thing that changed was the religion of the ruling dynasties. This periodization became axiomatic to the interpretation of Indian history. It also had a major political fallout effect in the twentieth century when the subcontinent was partitioned on the basis of the supposed two nations defined by religion. Although discarded by historians, those that still hold to the theory continue to support the required hostility between Hindus and Muslims.

The second assertion was that the pre-colonial political economy conformed to the model of what was called Oriental Despotism. This again assumed a static society, characterized by an absence of private property in land, despotic and oppressive rulers and, therefore, endemic poverty. This pattern, commonly applied to Asian societies, did not envisage any marked economic change. A static society also meant that it lacked a sense of history.

The third aspect was that Hindu society had always been divided into four main castes—the varnas. This division, it was argued, was based on Indian society being a collection of segregated races, with caste as the mechanism that controlled segregation through a code of regulations that determined how it was to function. Therefore, it remained unchanging through history. Racial identity was at the forefront in discussions on society at that time with the prevalence of what was called 'race science' in Europe. This notion of caste was derived by colonial scholars largely from what they saw as the Aryan foundations of Indian civilization, both as a race and a language.

The earlier people were labelled as Dravidian because of its being another ancient language with a distinct geographical location and substantial numbers of speakers. Dravidian became the counterpoint to the Aryan. Sanskrit was viewed as the dominant language of the Aryan civilization and the hegemonic religion was Vedic Brahmanism. In all three descriptions, India was projected as the alien, the 'Other' of Europe. Europe had to be projected as unique and Asia as lacking in the characteristics of European civilization.

Colonial interpretations claimed to be applying the criteria of Enlightenment rationality to their interpretation of the history of the colony. But, in effect, they were imposing a history that was not divorced from justifying colonial dominance. These preconceptions, together with a focus on chronology and the narrative of dynasties, governed routine history. Colonial historians drew on texts encapsulating the upper-caste perspectives of Indian society and extended it to the whole of society. Indian historians writing on ancient India came from the newly emerged middle class and were of the upper castes and therefore familiar with these texts. There may have been some hesitation in analysing their contents critically in the manner required by historical research, as among the texts were those often regarded as sacred. The colonial routine continued.

Nevertheless, a debate did emerge especially among historians influenced by nationalist ideas and opposed to some colonial preconceptions. The colonial periodization was generally accepted. A few changed the nomenclature to Ancient, Medieval and Modern, borrowed from Europe and thought to be more secular, although the markers remained the same and there was no effective change.

Oriental Despotism as a theory that explained the pre-modern political economy of India had few takers. Nationalist Indian historians largely rejected it. However, alternative hypotheses on the early Indian political economy and society were limited. This would have meant critiquing the normative texts and giving greater credence to non-religious texts. Social history in standard works largely reiterated the description of the four castes as given in the normative texts—the codes of caste society known as the Dharmashastras—registering little recognition of deviations, leave alone explaining them. Even where there was a conflict between the sacred text and inscriptional evidence, the conflict was not analysed and the textual statements were taken as correct. That the system need not have worked precisely as described in theory was not generally envisaged. Other ways of looking at the past were not admitted to the forefront of historical writing.

The predominant form of nationalism, described as anti-colonial and secular, was beginning to be imprinted on Indian historical writing in the early twentieth century. This was the nationalism of the majority of the Indian population. But parallel to this, and initially less apparent in historical writing, were emerging the two religious 'nationalisms'—Hindu and Muslim—much encouraged by the colonial version of the Indian past. These were not essentially anti-colonial since their agenda lay in their political ambition of establishing separate religion-based nation states. They were less interested in researching alternate paradigms and explanations of history and more in seeking to use history as given by colonial scholarship to legitimize their political ideology and the mobilization that they sought. There was an even greater insistence that a religious identity had always been the seminal identity in the past and continued to be so in the present. They argued that this identity of Hindu and Muslim would define the character of the nation states in contemporary times, even if it meant establishing two separate nations. Religion for them was more important than democracy and human rights. In the case of Hindu nationalism, the religion referred to is the religion of the upper castes, that in effect was the religion of the minority group within the count of those that called themselves Hindus.

From these two perspectives, history was directed towards justifying what was to be the outcome of independence—the partition of India into two states, one upholding Islam and the other encapsulating the struggle between those wanting a secular democracy and those proposing a Hindu state. The colonial view of Indian history was being echoed in these ideas. The argument that if the one came, the other was inevitable was only held by those who accepted the colonial version of Indian history as did the 'religious' nationalists, although they never admit to their sources. Post-colonial mainstream nationalism as different from the religious nationalisms still insisted that the state of India should be a secular democracy and that is what Indian nationalists had fought for.

Where nationalism based on a specific religious, linguistic or ethnic identity has been successful in creating a nation state, it is used to justify identity politics. The identities that fail to be dominant take on the characteristics of a kind of sub-nationalism until such time as they too aspire to the making of yet another nation, or else fall by the wayside. Identity need not always be derived from religion. With Bangladesh it was language. More recent but unsuccessful demands for nationhood, such as that of Khalistan among the Sikhs, stemmed again from religion within the context of a larger nation that is multi-religious.

Secessionist movements are not unknown even to well-established nations—such as Scottish nationalism—but they need not be violent or identified with an extremist ideology, although Irish nationalism, for obvious reasons, was different. In India there have been some trends in that direction with language-based movements in South India and demands for regional autonomy. Movements oriented more to ethnicity are known from the Northeast.

The colonial inheritance, where it remains unquestioned, persists, and religious nationalisms appropriate it and build on it. It dominates the thinking of those that regard themselves as defending all things Indian, by which they often mean Hindu, or else defending the religion they support and oppose the minority community from which non-compliance is feared. This is an explicit continuation of James Mill's two-nation theory with its insistence on the innate hostility between Hindus and Muslims, and the theory of the victimization of the Hindus by Muslim rulers. So the counterpart to Pakistan has to be a Hindu India according to some, even if a secular India is more viable, given the nation's history (and current reality) of multiple cultures and the plurality of religious beliefs.

The argument that a religion-based state, drawing on majority and minority religious communities as its units, militates against democracy is of little concern to such opinion. The undemocratic intentions of religion-based nationalisms are brushed aside by them and more so now that we are enmeshed in a neo-liberal market economy that reiterates hierarchies of inequality. Movements from below demanding equal rights are described as threats to the state.

Muslim religious nationalism demanded a separate state using the colonial argument of two nations and, according to some, such a state could have been the core of a rejuvenated Islamic world. Not all Muslim organizations in pre-Partition India supported this argument, and some opposed it; nevertheless it claimed, as religious nationalisms have to, that it had the support of the majority.

History, as viewed by Hindu religious nationalism in its incarnation as Hindutva, is a simple narrative of Hindus having been the original inhabitants of the land later known as British India, and therefore the rightful inheritors of the past. It is said that the Hindus once had a great and glorious past that was destroyed by Muslim conquerors. Consequently, the creation of a Hindu state is projected as a legitimate return to a rightful inheritance. The unbroken descent of Hindu ancestry and religion (pitribhumi and punyabhumi) from earliest times, according to this school of thought, legitimizes the primacy of the Hindus in the present. It combines with this the construction by Friedrich Max Müeller, the Orientalist and philologist, of a superior Aryan culture and the Aryan foundations of Indian (read Hindu) civilization.

Interestingly, it was the Theosophists, and in particular Colonel H. S. Olcott, the organization's co-founder, who were initially the major propagators of this theory in the nineteenth century. Olcott argued that the Aryans were indigenous to India and took civilization from India to the West, an idea that is promoted by Hindutva, but with no reference to its colonial origins. The Theosophists were close to the Arya Samaj for a while before they fell out.

The advantage of the Aryan theory of origins was that the upper caste claimed an Aryan descent and thereby also an unbroken lineage of dominance since the beginning of the establishment of civilization. They also claimed close kinship with the British who were geographically at the other end of the Aryan spread across Eurasia. The existence of the Harappan civilization discovered in the 1920s questions this narrative. But by maintaining that the Harappans were also Aryans this questioning is disallowed. However, there is as yet no evidence for this argument. Both the two-nation theory and the theory of Aryan origins are rooted in the nineteenth-century colonial interpretation of Indian history. These theories become a form of nurturing and continuing colonial explanations of Indian history, while claiming them as indigenous Indian history.

Most historians have questioned these and other theories formulated, for instance, by the trilogy of Mill-Macaulay-Müeller, the authors of the more established colonial construction of the Indian past. (Thomas Babington Macaulay was a British politician and administrator and the author of the infamous 1835

Minute on Indian Education that dismissed the 'whole native literature of India and Arabia' as worthless.) Ironically, the historians who have questioned these colonial theories are the ones who are accused by the Hindutva-vadis of being anti-national, the children of Macaulay, and 'Marxist'. The contemporary historical moment is that of a postcolonial state, an independent nation, and the conflict is over the immense change in power relations that this entails. The conflict is dressed up in the clothes of religion and the slogan is that the pre-eminence of Hindutva has to be established.

◆

Hindutva, the brand of Hinduism propagated by Hindu religious nationalists, is by definition not identical with Hinduism. As has been pointed out by many, whereas Hinduism is a religion, Hindutva is an ideology for political mobilization. I have elsewhere referred to Hindutva as Syndicated Hinduism. It draws on the Judeo-Christian religions in terms of hierarchical organizations and attempts to have a creed of belief, which is why some prefer to describe it as the semitization of Hinduism. Up to a point, the difference can be demonstrated in the relationship of Hindutva to Hinduism. Hinduism is a mosaic of belief systems, some linked, others not. Hindutva has the characteristics of a sect that reformulates selected beliefs to create, in this case, a socio-political organization with an attempt at ideological coherence. This is why it contests ideas that either question its ideology or allow it to be modified or adapted. Its political function is primary.

The term Hindutva was invented in this sense by V. D. Savarkar in 1923 and was adopted by the Bharatiya Janata Party (BJP) as its ideology in 1989. Therefore, not all Hindus are or need be supporters of Hindutva despite the assumption of the latter that they are. As a belief system, Hinduism accommodates a range of beliefs and sometimes there could even be ambivalence about non-belief. The sect, in contrast, has always had a particular definition that its followers observe, as with Hindutva. So far, those identified with Hindutva have tended to be viewed as a minority group within the majority community of the religion, Hinduism. This could, of course, change. Does Hindutva lack the confidence and security of actually being the majority community despite its claims?

The need to resort to threats, violence and vandalism by some groups of the Sangh Parivar that claim to be guided by Hindutva ideas remains inexplicable since the majority community in whose name they function is overwhelmingly large in numbers. There is absolutely no need to terrorize others. There are some obvious reasons for using intimidation on the general public that may provide some explication: to ensure that the majority gives its unalloyed political support to one party by raising the call that the religion is threatened; by disallowing a level playing field in the belief that doing so would no longer give an advantage to the majority; to prevent the erosion of the social code of caste and patriarchy; the apprehension that the nation may take upon itself the task of establishing a secular democracy—as was the intention initially—and thus deny automatic authority to the religious majority.

Religions in India, however, are not of the same mould as the Judeo-Christian ones. To recognize the difference would require that the pattern of religious organizations, how they affected society and also reflected it, and the history of the interaction of religions in India would have to be studied as a complement to the study of textual traditions and theology. One obvious example of this is the manner in which caste and religious sects interacted, each affecting the other and creating links of a kind not paralleled in most other parts of the world.

On the face of it, the relations between religion and society in the cultures of India and China were different from Europe, as indeed they were different from each other. So the specificity of the culture, the way its religion related to its society, as well as its historical context, all these factors imprinted the form it took. We have to see how and why they differed, what was specifically Indian about its religion, and the nature of its interface with society. We have tended to study the texts and theologies of the religions without giving sufficient attention to analysing the social institutions and enterprises and sectarian and community observances that the religions gave rise to, or on which they had an impact.

This would need an analysis of the history of religions in India as part of the pattern of life of the society, and not just as a history of their respective texts. Religious organizations that run religious institutions such as temples, mosques, churches and gurdwaras, as well as schools and other educational institutions have to be assessed in terms of their social functions apart from the religious, and for their efficiency in these functions. It was claimed that social codes, such as the *Manava Dharmashastra* (popularly referred to as the *Manusmriti*) and the Islamic Shari'a, had divine sanction, but these were drawn up and imposed by human sanction, and were and are liable to change. Practices do not necessarily follow the code but the code is quoted to restrict the autonomy of society and for retaining control over it by religious authority.

Even if one accepts the divine origin of religious belief, the activity associated with a religion lies in the hands of its human devotees and has to be seen as its history, as all else is seen. How did this interaction vary from sect to sect or across sects of the various religions practised in India? New needs led to the creation of new sects. What came to be called Hinduism in later times was, in essence, the juxtaposition of a large number of sects with their own focus of worship and ritual, some tied in to caste and inevitably reflecting some of the differences associated with caste, and some negating it.

This explains in part why a geographical term came to be used later for a collection of religious sects. The term 'Hindu', used in West Asia, was derived from 'Sindhu' and the Old Iranian 'Hindush', referring to the River Indus. It initially designated a geographical area—the land to the east of the Indus as viewed by those in West Asia. The label came to be applied to people who lived there, and finally to the religions practised by them, for which there was no single name. For many centuries the sects chose the deity they wished to worship, the form of worship and the text that they regarded as sacred.

There was no single sacred text since Hindu sects were not religions of the book. But today the Bhagavad Gita is being described as the 'national' book, with the suggestion that it be taught in every school, which, apart from anything else, conflates nationalism with religion, despite their being distinct. And if we are going to collapse the two, then logically there will be a demand that in a multi-religious state we must also declare the Quran, the Bible, the Guru Granth Sahib, the Avesta, and the books sacred to other religious communities as national books. Would the secular nature of Indian democracy then be tied to a library of religious books? Surely, they can be taught in school not as 'national' books but as the respected texts of various religions, which, in effect, is what they are.

Religious sects, as different from a monolithic religion, tend to shade off from the very orthodox to those far less so. This allows greater flexibility and fluidity in belief and practice among them than is normal in a religion treated as a monolithic entity.

The varied sects of Vaishnavas, Shaivas, Shaktas, and the Bhakti and Sufi sects, and many others, did not conform to a single church, nor were they governed by a single ecclesiastical authority. The change from sect to monolithic religion changes the nature of the relationship between religion and society.

Conversion, for most of these individual sects, was an alien idea. Opting out of the sect one identified with could also affect one's caste identity, and a person without a caste identity was regarded as an outcaste, and of little consequence in the larger society. A caste identity would continue if a caste as a collective converted, as often happened in conversions to Islam or Christianity. All religions in India, irrespective of their theoretical support of social equality, maintained caste distinctions—especially in the codes of marriage and inheritance.

This was also demonstrated to a more marked extent in the universal segregation of Dalit groups across all religions. Because much of religion was also linked to caste, it was not surprising that Christianity and Islam in India also functioned through a variety of sects, and recognized caste inequality and hierarchy in practice, however much they may have disavowed it in theory. This link often encouraged an overlap or closeness between various sects as in the dialogues between Sufi and Bhakti sects. If the way in which society is observed were to change and the view from the Dalit perspective was to be taken, then it would refer to a far larger expanse of society with segregation and ghettoization as its main characteristic. This is a very different view from that of the Brahmanas or of the distinctive upper-caste religions.

Since there were no monolithic religious communities of Hindus and Muslims organized across regions with a subcontinental base, there was little consciousness of it at an all-India level as there is now. It also explains why, when there was disagreement and conflict over religious belief and practice, the hostilities were largely limited to local sectarian confrontations. The Chola rulers, it seems, were unaware of Mahmud of Ghazni's raids on wealthy Hindu temples and the threat that this might have posed to Hinduism even though the Cholas were contemporaries of the Ghaznavids.

The devotional cults, sometimes referred to as Bhakti, in their early phase had similar but not identical manifestations in different parts of the subcontinent in the thousand years from the seventh to the seventeenth centuries CE. The later manifestations in each area show little recognition of earlier forms in neighbouring areas, although the message being propagated and the hymns sung by these 'sants' were not so dissimilar. Was this only because of the difference in regional language? This earlier kind of religious articulation allowed religion to be relatively more tolerant, as religions go, although the orthodox did not refrain from hostility against what were regarded as heretical sects.

Central to the social structure was the inexcusable social intolerance as expressed in the exclusion and oppression of all non-caste groups, the Adivasis, lower castes and Dalits. The exclusion, often ignored by quoting the texts that do not pointedly refer to it, is evident however in descriptions of social practice. As I've said earlier in this essay, and elsewhere, when caste Hindus today speak of their supposed victimization by Muslims for a thousand years, do they pause to think of the tyranny to which they subjected Dalits and Adivasis for over two millennia? The victimization of human beings by treating them as untouchable is worse than any other. The Hindu codes sanctioned this victimization. How do upper-caste Muslims and Christians reconcile their discrimination against Muslim and Christian Dalits, a discrimination that was contrary to their religious teachings where all men are said to be equal in the eyes of God? Why do we not ask Dalits and Adivasis what nationalism means to them? Do they even know that as Indian citizens they are entitled to human rights and social justice? Or have they been told by local authorities that nationalism means waving flags and shouting slogans on specific occasions?

The interweaving of religions and social forms, both of the past and the present, needs investigation. I have often said that the history of religion in Indian culture is distinctively different from what it has been in other cultures, and certainly from that of the West. Instead of investigating the difference, evaluating its nuances, and assessing how it related to the needs of those who supported it, as is required in the study of every religion, there is a tendency that it be seen as, and be converted into, a particular mould—similar to the Semitic religions as many have commented— emphasizing the power of religious organizations and hostility against those that contested its power. This does little justice to what was in many ways an interestingly different religious articulation in history and to understanding its relation to a social structure that was specific to India.

Texts too should be read with reference to their context. How did religious sects interact with social groups and how and why did they change when they did? Such an exploration would reveal the reality of the practice of a religion and not leave us imagining a reality. Hurt religious sentiments—irrespective of the religion they refer to—are equally an articulation of a rejection of contemporary rational thinking as of an objection to the thwarting of the past practices of the particular religion.

◆

It is not my intention to touch upon all the areas that concern the concept, definition and origins of Indian nationalism, but largely to suggest that intentions and ideologies should be viewed with clarity when we consider the links we make between religion, politics and society. We have yet to learn that the demands of democratic functioning can be met perfectly well without the intervention of religion. Religion belongs to a different sphere of life. Even to maintain a viable democracy there would have to be much more discussion of its essentials. To have insisted on adult franchise was an excellent decision but we need to go further in establishing institutions that support democracy and in questioning the continuation of colonial ideas that conflict with democracy. A distribution of wealth that negates the continuance of poverty and the protection of social justice are two essentials of democratic functioning. These are the kinds of rights endorsed by a secular society and are prime requirements in a nationalist ideology. Religious identities determining social institutions can conflict with the secular and the absence of the latter makes society less democratic. If these issues and their implications can be openly debated without fear of being silenced and the threat of assassination, it will make for a more vibrant society.

Among the issues that are important to the understanding of nationalism as the ideology that defines a nation are territory, democracy, culture, human rights and social justice. Territorial boundaries are not permanent. Nations do attempt to keep the boundaries intact but this is not guaranteed. If sub-nationalism takes on the dimensions of nationalism, the area of territorial control can be affected. Territories situated on the borders are the most vulnerable as we know from our own experience since 1947.

Democracy is fundamental to our country

as a modern nation and it has to be a secular democracy. This runs into problems with religious and caste-based nationalisms that give priority to particular communities. This is counter to the basis of nationalism. Safeguarding democracies means disallowing such priorities on the understanding that social and economic rights are written into the system.

We are still in the process of internalizing, as it were, the essential institutions required for democratic functioning. Continuities from the colonial tradition—as in some of our laws—need to be assessed and where they are anachronistic (as many are) they need to be changed. The law referring to sedition is one such. Speaking against the British colonial government, even without inciting violence against it, was enough to be considered as seditious. In a free country, criticizing the government is not an act of sedition nor can it be regarded as anti-national. It should be accepted as the right of every citizen. There are many aspects of the penal code that need to be assessed in our changed circumstances of being a free nation and, if thought to be unnecessary, removed from the legal code. The presence of such legislation unnecessarily allows governments to act in a dictatorial manner.

Democracy without its complement of secular

thinking falls short of being a democracy. Secular thinking has to induct degrees of rationality and logic as ways of thinking and more so if it is to be a qualifier for democracy. Let me reiterate that a democracy ceases to be so if it is governed by permanent majoritarian identities of any kind. This is not a matter of religion versus secularism, but rather of how and where such identities become increasingly a threat.

Whereas in the past religions practised in the subcontinent have been enmeshed in the social institutions of caste, this is now undergoing change, as is caste itself. Where it is playing new roles, as in vote banks and educational reservations, its links to religion are likely to create other problems. In earlier times the state bestowed its patronage on any or all religions, now this will have to be withdrawn in a secular society. The adjustment in India is not limited to the dual role of what has been called 'the Church' versus 'the State', but requires a revision of what had been the triangular relationship between the state, religions and castes. Where religion is so closely tied to caste this becomes a matter of central importance. A secular democracy, once it is established, makes no concession to caste or religion. We haven't arrived there yet but we have to be clear about this as we strive to get there.

Cultures or the patterns of living in a society are varied but have integral relationships that are intrinsic to nationalism. We tend to identify with the culture of the elite upper castes, and ignore that of the marginalized groups. But national culture has also to integrate the culture of the underprivileged. This does not mean a reshuffling of all cultures to arrive at a uniform pattern. It means that at least there should be the juxtaposition of cultures with interconnections so that some are not swept aside. The interconnections are often the clue to cultural norms and these in turn are significant in assessing a nation. It is all too easy to define elite cultures as the national culture but this misses the point of defining national culture as all-inclusive. Recognizing the range of cultures is crucial to the meaning of nationalism as is that of recognizing those that are catalysts.

What we most easily understand by cultural nationalism has stayed close to the contours dictated by colonial preconceptions. The claims frequently made by groups today to authentic, indigenous identities, unchanging and eternal, pose immense problems for historians, as they are often rooted in colonial readings of the past. Identities are neither timeless and unchanging, nor homogenous, nor singular, as maintained in the nineteenth century notion of civilization. Cultural nationalism draws on ancient history. Understanding the construction of this particular nationalism requires familiarity with pre-modern history, although those that claim it frequently lack expertise in its study. Cultural nationalism does not mean the imposition of the culture of the majority community on society but the search for an integral cultural articulation that includes the range of communities.

I have been trying to question some of the identities with which we live and which some regard as historically valid. I have tried to argue that those identities that have conditioned some aspects of our lives in South Asia or are now being held out as determining our national future should be re-assessed to ascertain their validity. There is a need for recognizing that they may not be rooted in history but in other extraneous factors. And we have to remember that when history changes, identities also change. If the premises of the identity are no longer viable, can we continue to refer to them by the same label? Such monitoring involves a dialogue among historians and scholars but also, and importantly, between them and citizens.

We don't have to go far to understand what this implies as it is well within our own traditions. Religion as dharma was defined as two streams—Brahmanism and Shramanism. The first derived from Vedic Brahmanism and the second from Buddhism, Jainism, Ajivika teaching and various others. They held distinctly opposed views and yet the more worthwhile aspects of ancient culture and thought emerged from the existence of the two. The Bhakti tradition of medieval times inherited some of these ways and also interacted with Sufi ideas to create another kind of ambience that became characteristic of those times and encouraged further interactions at many levels. The colonial intervention gave us a new definition of our cultures and these we have to sift in terms of which definitions are feasible and which are colonial creations whose validity for contemporary times can be questioned.

The same process would apply to literature. What are the categories of texts and what has been their impact on our ways of thought? The impact might differ from language to language and, given its long history and multiple languages, we still have much to learn. The first language to be widely used, judging from the inscriptions scattered all over the subcontinent, was Prakrit. How did it evolve and what was the culture of those that first used it? The same kinds of questions would have to be asked of the many facets of what we collectively call cultures.

These are aspects to which we have to give attention when we speak of nationalism. But we often overlook other equally crucial aspects in the definition that are incorporated with a view to protecting and ensuring the entitlements to food, water, health care, education, employment and protection by law and state agencies that are the legitimate claim of every citizen. Nations in which there are huge distances between those that have these and those that do not—such nations don't fit easily into the best category of nations. Yet these basic entitlements are the essential requirements of nationhood. There cannot be a sense of community if the differences in society—economic and social—are vast. This is what needed attention at the start of our becoming an independent nation. Some effort was made in the initial years but there has been a gradual falling off and now between a third to half the people are hovering at the poverty line. How can impoverished, drought-ridden communities be concerned about the well-being of the 'the nation' when their livelihood is so insecure and their future so uncertain? But even a century ago when they were also impoverished, they were nevertheless committed to a secular nationalism and this was foundational to the making of the nation. We have to ask ourselves why it went no further.

To conclude on a personal note, these thoughts came to me again and again in the past few months. There has been so much talk about who is national and who is anti-national and those in authority insist that it is all about the kinds of slogans that one has to shout to avoid being called anti-national. But slogans do not make for nationalism or anti-nationalism. There has to be something more substantial to give hope to those that live at the edge of nowhere, that there is a reality that makes up a nation, and that this reality will take them away from the edge and bring them to the centre and make life worthwhile. It can be done but there has to be a will to do it. There has to be a reordering of priorities.

Among those that shall inherit this land, its cultures and its problems, there are some who are aware of this. These are issues that are foremost in the minds of students, perhaps more so among Dalit students. We heard them raise these issues at Jawaharlal Nehru University (JNU) and other universities. They were not just shouting slogans. They were demanding a different society, a society that ensured human rights and justice for all—precisely the kind of society that converts a country into a nation.

Speaking at the teach-in at JNU in March 2016, I was reminded of three experiences in my life linked to what is happening to us today as teachers and students. One was the discussions that were raised in the 1960s in many Indian universities about the kind of nation we wanted to build and what were to be its parameters. There was much thought on economic growth and on reducing the inequities of caste as a first step to removing them. The two streams of thought were interlinked. The discussions assumed the right to a complete freedom of expression when discussing all aspects of the nation—its weaknesses and its strengths. This freedom was respected as it generally is when it is given. The future of Kashmir was not treated with kid gloves.

Then I was reminded of the start of JNU in 1971. Ideas across the board went back and forth in the sorting out of courses and syllabi, with the Vice Chancellor of the university encouraging us to think of interdisciplinary courses and of not just repeating what was being taught in other universities. This we did achieve and it marked a new departure in the study of history, among other disciplines, as a social science in India. We also worked out as a university our own set of admission procedures with some small concessions to underprivileged students from economically backward areas, and what a dramatic change this made to the ambience of the university and to student-faculty relations.

It was not all smooth sailing. We had many gheraos of the Vice Chancellor and of individual faculty members, and we all took these gheraos and strikes in our stride. The issues ranged from student representation in the administrative bodies and student participation in deciding on courses to be taught, to statements on the malfunctioning of the government when it came to matters regarding education and even other matters of policy. The issues have hardly changed over the last half-century although students and teachers at universities have frequently and freely discussed them. But now the attitude of those in authority has changed. Perhaps it is their insecurity and lack of confidence that has terminated the possibility of free discussion.

At that time those teaching in Indian universities were well aware of the student protests that had virtually swept across the world since 1968. There was turmoil, there were demands for a different kind of course structure and student representation in university bodies. The students joined up with organizations of workers and of the poor, the demands took account of not just the kind of education they were getting and the courses they were being taught, but also included the kind of society they were living in.

There were barricades in Paris manned by students and faculty and there were clashes with the police. There was at the same time much discussion between students, faculty and administration, sometimes acrimonious and sometimes persuasive. What are today described in India as anti-national opinions were plentiful at the sit-ins at these universities and open to debate. Finally, changes were made in teaching and courses to accommodate some of the new ideas suggested and subsequently some student and faculty demands were introduced, and some rejected. The notion of sit-ins and teach-ins and extensive serious discussions was central to the process of learning and living in society.

That was one aspect of the nurturing of nationalism. It was turbulent but it encapsulated some of the changes that in retrospect one realizes were necessary. And further that it is imperative that universities provide the space and the opportunity for free discussion. Open minds and thoughtful minds are essential to the enterprise called nation-building.

A small tremor of this movement was also felt in Delhi University where I was then teaching. One of the forms it took was discussions among faculty and students about the nature of the revolution in Naxalbari that had just begun. We all knew therefore who the faculty and students were who were involved in these debates and those that supported this new form of self-expression as well as those who opposed it. Anxious parents would ask us to wean their children away from these radical ideas but we knew that this was an essential part of learning to think. The more open the discussion the better. The place for arguing about the validity of revolution was not prison, but university. Arguments should not be confined to secret cells but should be made openly. No one suggested closing down the university and sending faculty and students to prison. Vice Chancellors and governments knew, and had the confidence to know, that the best place for the young to talk about such problems was the university. Today, it seems those in authority think first of arresting students and faculty, charging them with sedition, and sending them to prison. All this for daring to discuss issues that are contrary to government policy. They are then punished with heavy fines and rustication. Some public personalities even demand the shutting down of the university. Are we living in the twenty-first century?

We have to decide today whether as citizens our commitment to the nation is to shout trite slogans required of us by people whose concern is largely that of acquiring power through current politics, and to dismiss as anti-national those that do not shout these slogans? Or whether we should reaffirm our faith in the nation by looking at how we can make it a society that is viable for every citizen, a society that stands by secular democratic values, that ensures a livelihood for everyone, and that defends and protects the right of every citizen to social justice. The latter would seem to be the more attractive future for our country.

The choice is ours.

NATIONALISM
AND
ITS CONTEMPORARY
DISCONTENTS
IN INDIA

———

A. G. NOORANI

In the 1950s, American senator Joseph McCarthy became notorious for his vicious attacks on the character and patriotism of his fellow Americans. In our country today we are witnessing similar irresponsible attacks on the patriotism and nationalism of citizens. These attacks are usually carried out by members of the Sangh Parivar, including those belonging to the ruling party. In this essay I would like to look at two aspects of this dangerous phenomenon: the law dealing with sedition, and the origins of the slogan 'Bharat Mata ki Jai'.

I
THE LAW OF SEDITION

The history of India's freedom movement is the history of the law of sedition in India and its systematic use by the British colonial rulers as a weapon to crush the freedom movement. That history is studded with notable trials of its leaders on charges of sedition. When India became independent, its leaders expressed their loathing of this law that the British had maliciously inscribed on the statute book.

None expressed the sentiment better than the first and greatest prime minister of the country—Jawaharlal Nehru. He said in Parliament on 29 May 1951: 'Take again Section 124A of the Indian Penal Code. Now so far as I am concerned that particular section is highly objectionable and obnoxious and it should have no place both for practical and historical reasons, if you like, in any body of laws that we might pass. The sooner we get rid of it the better. We might deal with that matter in other ways, in more limited ways, as every other country does but that particular thing, as it is, should have no place, because all of us have had enough experience of it in a variety of ways and apart from the logic of the situation, our urges are against it.'

Nevertheless, in 1962, the Supreme Court of independent India upheld Section 124A of the penal code, which defines the offence of sedition, albeit with a tortuous proviso that made no sense (as we shall see a little later in the Kedar Nath case). It is deeply worrying that in 2016 the BJP government, headed by Narendra Modi, should use Section 124A to imprison student leaders and prosecute political leaders.

The raison d'etre of Section 124A was stated all

too clearly in a definitive work on the subject, *A Treatise on the Law of Sedition and Cognate Offences in British India, Penal and Preventive* by W. R. Donogh. Donogh, a barrister who practised in the Calcutta High Court, laid bare his motivation at the very outset in his preface. 'If an apology be needed for the production of a work of this character, it might be possible to justify it on two grounds. One is the prominence which political offences of this type have assumed in India; the other, the importance of the preventive legislation recently introduced on the Statute-book, which, without prejudice to previously existing measures in *pari materia*, aims at a better control of the Platform and the Press... The present work has been designed to accomplish this object.'

COLONIALISM AND RACISM

Section 124A had once been Section 113 of Thomas Babington Macaulay's Draft Penal Code of 1837, but it was omitted in the Indian Penal Code when it was enacted in 1860. It was introduced through an amending bill by the Law Member of the Governor General's Executive Council, Sir James Fitzjames

Stephen, on 2 August 1870. He said: 'This law was substantially the same as the law of England at the present day, though it was much compressed, much more distinctly expressed, and freed from a great amount of obscurity and vagueness with which the law of England was hampered.' He then went on to state how the law of England stood on this subject. 'It consisted of three parts. There was, first, the Statute, commonly called the Treason-Felony Act (II Vic., c.12); secondly, the Common Law with regard to seditious libels; and thirdly, the law as to seditious words…'

Section 124A of the Indian Penal Code was, thus, deeply rooted in English law as its very language reveals: 'Whoever…brings or attempts to bring into hatred or contempt, or excites or attempts to excite disaffection towards the government established by law in India, shall be punished with imprisonment for life…or with imprisonment which may extend to three years plus fine.'

The features deserve note. First, no democratic government with any self-respect would demand the affection of its citizens; ruling monarchs do. English law has its origin in the days when the monarch ruled as well as reigned, though it persisted even after he had ceased to rule. Sedition was a short step away from treason. Secondly, the provision of imprisonment for life reveals the colonial rulers' mindset. Its purpose was to crush Indian rebels. To Stephen, the phrase 'liberty of the Press' was mere rhetoric. As a small mercy, comments expressing disapprobation of official acts and policies were permitted by Section 124A but with a proviso: those comments must not arouse any of the dreaded emotions it listed.

This became law on 25 November 1870. It was made even more stringent on 18 February 1898 as a result of Justice Arthur Strachey's ruling on Section 124A in the first Bal Gangadhar Tilak case (*Queen Empress vs Bal Gangadhar Tilak*). On 25 December 1897, a bill was moved by M. D. Chalmers to amend the general laws relating to sedition and cognate offences 'so as to make it efficient for its purposes'. The mover of the bill said: 'Then it is urged that the proposed clause goes further than English law, and again some passages in Sir Fitzjames Stephen's speech are referred to. All I can say is this. If in 1870 he thought that an appeal to force was a necessary constituent of sedition, he afterwards changed his mind... I take it that the offence is complete, both in India and England, if it be proved that the offender has attempted to excite disaffection towards the government. It is not necessary that he should himself appeal to force. What he does is to excite or attempt to excite feelings of discontent which make people ready for mischief should the opportunity arise.

'But after all, these arguments are more or less academic. No one in his senses would contend that because a given law is good and suitable in England, it is therefore good and suitable in India. If a rule of law exists in England we may fairly consider whether it is suitable to India, but the answer to the question must always depend on the conditions which prevail in India. How much licence of speech can be safely allowed is a question of time and place. If I smoke a cigar on the maidan it pleases me, and hurts no one else. If I smoke a cigar in the powder magazine of the Fort, I endanger the lives of many, and do an act well deserving punishment. Language may be tolerated in England which it is unsafe to tolerate in India, because in India it is apt to be transformed into action instead of passing off as harmless gas. In legislating for India we must have regard to Indian conditions, and we must rely mainly on the advice of those who speak under the weight of responsibility and have the peace and good government of India under their charge.'

The Lieutenant Governor of Bengal, Sir Alexander Mackenzie, said: 'It is clear that a sedition law which is adequate for a people ruled by a government of its own nationality and faith may be inadequate, or in some respects unsuited, for a country under foreign rule and inhabited by many races, with diverse customs and conflicting creeds. It is impossible in India to accept the test of direct incitement to violence or intention to commit rebellion, and limit the interference of the government to such cases. It is not the apparent intention of the writers or speakers so much as the tendency of the writings or speeches which has to be regarded, and the cumulative effect of depreciatory declamation on the minds of an ignorant and excitable population has to be taken into consideration.'

Thus, Section 124A is rooted not only in colonialism but also in racism.

In his treatise, Donogh reproduced with enthusiastic approval opinions by other colonial figures in India to the same effect, namely that Indians were an 'ignorant and excitable people'—an outlook shared, doubtless, by those who slap charges of sedition on university students and political opponents.

PROGRESSIVELY DRACONIAN

Originally, Section 124A penalized excitement of 'disaffection' alone. The 1898 amendment added 'hatred or contempt'. The warning was clear—you must neither hate the British rulers nor despise them. This is the form in which Section 124A still exists on our statute book. Strachey had warned: 'Disaffection may be excited in a thousand different ways. A poem, an allegory, a drama, a philosophical or historical discussion, may be used for the purpose of exciting disaffection just as much as direct attacks upon the government. You have to look through the form, and look to the real object: you have to consider whether the form of a poem or discussion is genuine, or whether it has been adopted merely to disguise the real seditious intention of the writer.' Following this verdict was a spate of repressive press legislation.

The mere mention of the word 'sedition' aroused in Indians the very emotions of hatred and contempt for the British that Section 124A sought to forbid. Emotions or opinions cannot be stifled by legislation. The trials for sedition that followed further aroused nationalist feelings.

Tilak's trial stirred people as none before and since

had. Defiance came naturally to this brave man. His first trial was in 1897 before Justice Strachey and a jury. Strachey held that mere excitement or attempt to excite the forbidden emotions sufficed to constitute sedition 'even if there is nothing to show that he succeeded' or that 'any disturbance' was caused. His ruling was upheld by the Privy Council. Tilak was sentenced to eighteen months' rigorous imprisonment.

The second trial for sedition was in 1908 before Justice D. D. Davar, who had been his counsel in the first trial, and a jury of which seven Europeans returned a verdict of guilty while the two Indians, both Parsis, returned a verdict of not guilty. Justice Davar sentenced Tilak to six years' transportation. At his third and last trial for sedition in 1916, he was successfully defended by Muhammad Ali Jinnah. Tilak had been ordered to execute a bond for Rs 20,000 'for good behaviour' for 'disseminating seditious matter'. Justices Batchelor and Shah quashed the order.

In 1891, opinion in Bengal was outraged by the prosecution for sedition of the editor, owner, printer and publisher of the newspaper *Bangobasi,* Jogendra Chandra Bose. It had trenchantly criticized the Governor General for the Age of Consent Bill as being offensive to Hindu sentiment. This divided Indian opinion because some welcomed the bill, opposed though they were to British rule. The jury was divided (7-2). The Chief Justice discharged the jury. 'This is not the case on which I should accept anything but an [*sic*] unanimous verdict.' The thousand-strong crowd of 'natives' cheered the result. But the accused apologized to the Government of India for their 'intemperate' language and the matter was dropped.

'SEDITION' AND INDIAN NATIONALISM

It was a great moment in the history of India's struggle for freedom when Maulana Mohammed Ali, Maulana Shaukat Ali and the Shankaracharya of Sharada Peeth were tried jointly in 1921 at Karachi for sedition, as well as other charges, at the height of the Khilafat Movement. Convicted, the Ali Brothers were released from prison in 1923. In 1922 Maulana Abul Kalam Azad's trial for sedition became famous for his magnificent statement in which he hurled defiance at the rulers. It was 'an oration deserving penal servitude for life', Gandhi wrote in *Young India* on 23 February 1922.

Gandhi's own trial for sedition in 1922 at

Ahmedabad became a legend for two reasons. First, for his open and full admission of responsibility for 'the diabolical crimes of Chauri Chaura or the mad outrages of Bombay'. Next, for the District and Sessions Judge C. N. Broomfield's generous remarks while pronouncing the sentence: 'It will be impossible to ignore the fact that you are in a different category from any person I have ever tried or am likely to have to try. It would be impossible to ignore the fact that in the eyes of millions of your countrymen you are a great patriot and a great leader. Even those who differ from you in politics look upon you as a man of high ideals and of noble and of even saintly life.'

Broomfield went on to become a highly respected judge of the Bombay High Court. (Some accounts of the case erroneously claim that the judge who tried Gandhi was 'Justice Strangman'. Sir Thomas Strangman, the Advocate General, was appointed Special Prosecutor in the case.)

These trials and others for graver offences—such as that of Aurobindo Ghose in the Alipore Bomb case (1908)—moulded public opinion. Trials create drama and trials for sedition involved the tallest figures. People hated the law of sedition that put them in peril. Sir Maurice Gwyer, the first Chief Justice of the Federal Court and a committed liberal, spurned the Strachey amendment and sought to inject the condition that 'reasonable anticipation or likelihood of public disorder is the gist of the offence'. It was a brave and well-meant effort. But the Privy Council, an instrument of colonial control, overruled him. The viceroy, Lord Linlithgow, so hated Sir Maurice that he asked London to send a King's Counsel to brainwash the Chief Justice. (Sir Maurice stayed on in India as the Vice Chancellor of Delhi University.)

This was the state of the law on sedition that the British rulers had imposed on the country before Independence. Indian opinion on the law was reflected in a pamphlet published by the Foreign Department of the All India Congress Committee (AICC). Written by Ram Manohar Lohia, it was entitled *The Struggle for Civil Liberties* and had a foreword by Jawaharlal Nehru. Lohia wrote: 'The ordinary law of sedition, Sea Customs Act and the Board of Censors are in themselves sufficient to put a ban on all advanced opinion, thought and art.'

The framers of India's Constitution proceeded warily, only to arrive at a sound conclusion. The Draft Report of the Constituent Assembly's Advisory Committee on Minorities, Fundamental Rights, etc., dated 3 April 1947, mentioned sedition among the grounds on which freedom of speech and expression may be restricted. The Drafting Committee also retained this ground later in 1947. In October 1948, it recommended the replacement of the words 'or undermines the authority or foundation of the state' in Clause 2 with the words 'or undermines the security of or tends to overthrow the state'. On 3 October 1947, the Drafting Committee had retained sedition as an offence in the Constitution. As did the Draft Constitution published in February 1948.

K. M. MUNSHI'S ROLE

It is to the credit of Drafting Committee member K. M. Munshi that he secured the deletion of sedition when the Constituent Assembly debated the Draft Constitution on 1 December 1948. Moving his amendment for its deletion, he said: 'The word "sedition" has been a word of varying import and has created considerable doubt in the minds of not only the members of this House but of courts of law all over the world. Its definition has been very simple and given so far back as 1868. It says "sedition embraces all those practices whether by word or deed or writing which are calculated to disturb the tranquillity of the state and lead ignorant persons to subvert the government". But in practice it has had a curious fortune. A hundred and fifty years ago in England, holding a meeting or conducting a procession was considered sedition. Even holding an opinion against, which will bring ill-will towards government, was considered sedition once. Our notorious Section 124 A of Penal Code was sometimes construed so widely that I remember in a case a criticism of a District Magistrate was urged to be covered by Section 124 A. But the public opinion has changed considerably since and now that we have a democratic Government a line must be drawn between criticism of Government which should be welcome and incitement which would undermine the security or order on which civilized life is based, or which is calculated to overthrow the State. Therefore the word "sedition" has been omitted. As a matter of fact the essence of democracy is Criticism of Government. The party system, which necessarily involves an advocacy of the replacement of one government by another, is its only bulwark; the advocacy of a different system of government should be welcome because that gives vitality to a democracy.' His amendment was adopted. Accordingly, the Revised Draft Constitution of November 1949 omitted sedition by a deliberate, considered decision.

Article 19(2) of the Constitution as it originally stood read thus: 'Nothing in sub-clause (a) of clause (1) shall affect the operation of any existing law in so far as it relates to or prevents the state from making any law relating to libel, slander, defamation, contempt of court or any matter which offends against decency or morality or which undermines the security of, or tends to overthrow, the state.'

It was, however, amended by the Constitution (First Amendment) Act, 1951. Clause (2) now read: 'Nothing in sub-clause (a) of clause (1) shall affect the operation of any existing law, or prevent the state from making any law, in so far as such law imposes reasonable restrictions on the exercise of the right conferred by the said sub-clause in the interests of the security of the state, friendly relations with foreign states, public order, decency or morality, or in relation to contempt of court, defamation or incitement to an offence.' It was in support of this amendment that Nehru denounced sedition.

The amendment made some changes: (i) Three new grounds of restriction were introduced: (a) friendly relations with foreign states; (b) public order;

and (c) incitement to an offence. (ii) The ground 'tends to overthrow the state' was deleted. (iii) The words 'any matter which offends against or undermines the security of the state' were substituted by the words 'in the interests of the security of the state'. (iv) The words 'libel, slander' were dropped retaining only the generic term 'defamation'. (v) The qualification 'reasonable restrictions' was inserted to govern all the grounds.

In *Romesh Thapar vs State of Madras* (1950) Justice Patanjali M. Sastri said: 'It is also worthy of note that the word "sedition" which occurred in Art. 13(2) of the Draft Constitution prepared by the Drafting Committee was deleted before the article was finally passed as Art. 19(2)... Deletion of the word "sedition" from the draft Art. 13(2), therefore, shows that criticism of Government exciting disaffection or bad feelings towards it is not to be regarded as a justifying ground for restricting the freedom of expression and of the press, unless it is such as to undermine the security or tend to overthrow the State.'

The Press Commission's report noted the ruling of the Punjab High Court in Master Tara Singh's case in 1952. It was held that Section 124A had become void as contravening the right to freedom of speech and expression guaranteed by Article 19(1) and that the section was not saved by Article 19(2), under which only those utterances could be penalized which undermined the security of the state or tended to overthrow the state. Sir Eric Weston, the distinguished District and Sessions Judge, who in the course of his career rose to become one of the most respected judges of the Bombay High Court, and eventually the Chief Justice of the Punjab High Court, said in the course of the judgment, 'The section has become inappropriate by the very nature of the change which has come about, viz., India becoming a sovereign democratic state.' It recommended repeal of Section 124A. Headed by Justice G. S. Rajadhyaksha of the Bombay High Court, the Press Commission had among its members men of high stature such as C. P. Ramaswamy Iyer, Acharya Narendra Dev and Dr Zakir Hussain.

OMISSION OF 'SEDITION'

When the Constitution of India came into force on 26 January 1950, sedition did not figure in Article 19(2) among the grounds on which the fundamental right to freedom of speech and expression (Art. 19(1) (a)) could be subjected to 'reasonable restrictions' by law. Its history and case law suggested clearly that it could not be stretched to fall within 'public order' or 'incitement to an offence'. Sir Maurice Gwyer sought to do that albeit with good intentions. The Government of India Act, 1935, did not contain a Bill of Rights. He had to enforce the law of sedition against Indians, as Linlithgow desired. He chose another option, which was to 'read it down' and inject into Section 124A, by judicial fiat, the ingredient of incitement to public disorder. This, of course, was contrary to the intention of the framers of Section 124A, especially after its amendment in 1898, and was contrary to Justice Strachey's exposition, which had held sway for half a century. The Privy Council reversed Gwyer.

The author of Section 124A, Stephen, had noted that 'the Penal Code contained no provision at all as to seditious offences not involving an absolute breach of the peace'.

After the Constitution came into force, the High Courts did the correct thing—strike down Section 124A as being violative of Article 19(2). Courts exist to erase blots on the statute book. It is no function of a court of law to recycle statutory garbage. As early as in *Romesh Thapar vs State of Madras* Justice Sastri had drawn pointed attention to the deliberate omission of

sedition in the Constitution. That was message enough
for the High Courts. A full bench of three judges of the
Allahabad High Court unanimously held Section124A
to be void in *Ram Nandan vs State*. It comprised
Justices M. C. Desai, R. N. Gurtu and N. U. Beg,
each of whom wrote a judgment of considerable
learning and cogency of reasoning. No precedent,
English, American or Indian, was overlooked. Justice
Desai was against 'importing words in S.124A' and
held that 'the right to spread disaffection against the
government or any other person is included in the
right to freedom of speech and expression guaranteed
by the Constitution...danger to public order is not
an ingredient of the offence'. He also cited the Press
Commission's recommendation for its repeal.

Concurring, Justice Gurtu noted the omission of
'sedition' in Article 19(2), while Justice Beg surveyed
the legislative process which led to the enactment of
Section 124A in 1870 and its amendment in 1898.

THE KEDAR NATH SINGH CASE

Then, on 20 January 1962, came the judgment of
the Constitution Bench of the Supreme Court, in

Kedar Nath Singh vs State of Bihar. Kedar Nath Singh, a member of the Forward Communist Party, had delivered a speech nearly a decade earlier on 26 May 1953, in which he said: 'Today the dogs of the C.I.D. are loitering round Barauni. Many official dogs are sitting even in this meeting. The people of India drove out the Britishers from this country and elected these Congress goondas to the gaddi and seated them on it. The capitalists and the zamindars of this country help these Congress goondas. These zamindars and capitalists will also have to be brought before the people's court along with these Congress goondas.

'On the strength of the organisation and unity of kisans and mazdoors the Forward Communist Party will expose the black deeds of the Congress goondas, who are just like the Britishers. Only the colour of the body has changed. They have today established a rule of lathis and bullets in the country...

'The Forward Communist Party does not believe in the doctrine of vote itself. The party had always been believing in revolution and does so even at present. We believe in that revolution, which will come and in the flames of which the capitalists, zamindars and the Congress leaders of India, who have made it their profession to loot the country, will be reduced to ashes and on their ashes will be established a Government of the poor and the downtrodden people of India.

'It will be a mistake to expect anything from the Congress rulers. They (Congress rulers) have set up V[inoba] Bhave in the midst of the people by causing him to wear a langoti in order to divert the people's attention from their mistakes. Today [Vinoba] is playing a drama on the stage of Indian politics. Confusion is being created among the people... I want to tell the last word even to the Congress tyrants... Today the children of the poor are hankering for food and you (Congress-men) are assuming the attitude of Nawabs sitting on the chairs.'

He was sentenced to rigorous imprisonment for a year. There was nothing remotely seditious in the speech; not even the advocacy of revolution. There clearly was no immediate incitement to violent revolution.

A unanimous judgment delivered by Chief Justice B. P. Sinha remarked: 'This species of offence against the State was not an invention of the British Government in India, but has been known in England for centuries. Every State, whatever its form of Government, has to be armed with the power to punish those who, by their conduct, jeopardise the safety and stability of the State, or disseminate such feelings of disloyalty as have the tendency to lead to the disruption of the State or to public disorder. In England, the crime has thus been described by Stephen in his *Commentaries on the Laws of England...*'

Old English cases were relied on, as was Gwyer's ruling. These observations by the Supreme Court are noteworthy. 'Hence any acts within the meaning of S.124A which have the effect of subverting the Government by bringing that Government into contempt or hatred, or creating disaffection against it, would be within penal statute because the feeling of disloyalty to the Government established by law or enmity to it imports the idea of tendency to public disorder by the use of actual violence or incitement to violence. In other words, any written or spoken words, etc., which have implicit in them the idea of subverting Government by violent means, which are compendiously included in the term "revolution", have been made penal by the section in question.'

Thus the mere advocacy of revolution was sedition itself. 'But the freedom has to be guarded against becoming a licence for vilification and condemnation of the Government established by law, in words which incite violence or have tendency to create public disorder...bringing the law into line with the law of sedition in England, as was the intention of the legislators when they introduced S.124A into the Indian Penal Code in 1870 as aforesaid, the law will be within the permissible limits laid down in cl. (2) of Art.19 of the Constitution, if, on the other hand, we give a literal meaning to the words of the section, divorced from all the antecedent background in which the law of sedition has grown, as laid down in the several decisions of the Judicial Committee of the Privy Council, it will be true to say that the section is not only within but also very much beyond the limits laid down in cl. (2) aforesaid.'

The record shows this assertion to be untrue. Bar a perfunctory reference to Justice Sastri's observation, there was no discussion of the process by which the framers of the Constitution chose deliberately to omit sedition; no reference to the Press Commission's recommendation and, worst of all, no reference to the full bench ruling of the Allahabad High Court or to Nehru's speech in 1951 denouncing sedition—amidst copious quotes from old, obsolete English rulings.

An undergraduate whose essay on sedition contained blemishes such as these would earn a deserved reprimand. Kedar Nath's case passed muster and its baleful impact survived to poison the wells of free speech. Chief Justice Sinha's apologia betrayed his outlook and that of the other four judges: 'The species of offence against the state was not an invention of the British government in India, but has been known in England for centuries.'

Although the Kedar Nath Singh case was relied on unquestioningly in the first two examples below, acquittals took place because of the facts of the cases.

1. *Balwant Singh & ANR. vs State of Punjab* (1995). A liberal bench acquitted the appellant who had raised the slogans 'Khalistan Zindabad' and 'Raj Karega Khalsa' because 'no disturbance, whatsoever was caused'.

2. *Bilal Ahmed Kaloo vs State of Andhra Pradesh* (1997). The appellant was acquitted because he had not done 'anything against the Government of India or any other Government of the state'.

3. Kedar Nath Singh was not relied on in *Nazir Khan vs State of Delhi* (2003), but its spirit so possessed Justice Arijit Pasayat that he went so far as to say: 'Section 124-A deals with "Sedition". Sedition is a crime against society nearly allied to that of treason, and it frequently precedes treason by a short interval. Sedition in itself is a comprehensive

term, and it embraces all those practices, whether by word, deed, or writing, which are calculated to disturb the tranquillity of the State, and lead ignorant persons to endeavour to subvert the Government and laws of the country. The objects of sedition generally are to induce discontent and insurrection, and stir up opposition to the Government, and bring the administration of justice into contempt; and the very tendency of sedition is to incite the people to insurrection and rebellion. "Sedition" has been described as disloyalty in action, and the law considers as sedition all those practices which have for their object to excite discontent or dissatisfaction, to create public disturbance, or to lead to civil war; to bring into hatred or contempt the Sovereign or the Government, the laws or constitutions of the realm, and generally all endeavours to promote public disorder.'

US SUPREME COURT RULING

Illiberalism pervades the Supreme Court's rulings whenever its judges face the insecurity or dissent they dread—be it the Terrorist and Disruptive Activities (Prevention) Act (TADA), Prevention of Terrorism Act (POTA) or Armed Forces Special Powers Act (AFSPA). The law of sedition is in an unholy mess. Its import depends on the outlook of judges, which is none too liberal. Contrast these rulings with the unanimous ruling of the US Supreme Court in 1969 in *Brandenburg vs Ohio*. It concerned a Ku Klux Klan leader who shouted at a meeting, where others carried firearms, 'Bury the niggers', 'The niggers should be returned to Africa' and 'Send the Jews back to Israel'. The majority held that 'the constitutional guarantees of free speech and free press do not permit a State to forbid or proscribe advocacy of the use of force or of law violation except where such advocacy is directed to inciting or producing imminent lawless action and is likely to incite or produce such action. As we said in *Noto vs United States*, "the mere abstract teaching of the moral propriety or even more necessity for a resort to force and violence, is not the same as preparing a group for violent action and steeling it to such action". We are here confronted with a statute which, by its own words and as applied, purports to punish mere advocacy and to forbid, on pain of criminal punishment, assembly with others merely to advocate the described type of action. Such a statute falls within the condemnation of the First and Fourteenth Amendments.'

Concurring, Justice William Douglas asked: 'Suppose one tears up his own copy of the Constitution in eloquent protest to a decision of this court. May he be indicted? Suppose one rips his own Bible to shreds to celebrate his departure from one "faith" and his embrace of atheism. May he be indicted?'

Will one who burns the *Manusmriti* be indicted? What of Mayawati's attacks on manuwadis?

In *Hector vs Attorney-General of Antigua*, the Privy Council held: 'In a free democratic society it is almost too obvious to need stating that those who hold office in government and who are responsible for public administration must always be open to criticism. Any attempt to stifle or fetter such criticism amounts to political censorship of the most insidious and objectionable kind. At the same time it is no less obvious that the very purpose of criticism levelled at those who have the conduct of public affairs by their political opponents is to undermine public confidence in their stewardship and to persuade the electorate that the opponents would make a better job of it than those presently holding office. In the light of these considerations their Lordships cannot help viewing statutory provision which criminalises statements likely to undermine public confidence in the conduct of public affairs with the utmost suspicion. [I]t would on any view be a grave impediment to the freedom of the press if those who print, or a fortiori those who distribute, matter reflecting critically on the conduct of public authorities could only do so with impunity if they could first verify the accuracy of all statements of fact on which the criticism was based.'

These observations establish the fundamental fallacy underlying Chief Justice Sinha's logic—words cannot be read into a penal statute in order to validate it. Said the Privy Council: 'Their Lordships are willing to give full weight to the presumption of constitutionality but think that the attempt to contrive a suitable implied term in this context only serves to emphasise the inherent conflict between the provision which it is sought to rescue and the constitutional safeguards of free speech.'

ENGLISH HISTORY AND SEDITION

England's history is rich in trials for sedition, which shaped the country and bestirred its people.

The volumes of State Trials record the struggle for freedom of speech; most notably, in the magnificent speech by the greatest advocate of all time of this fundamental right, Sir Thomas Erskine, in defence of Thomas Paine's *The Rights of Man* in 1792.

In 1977, Britain's Law Commission recommended the abolition of the law of sedition. In 1984, Lord Alfred Denning expressed the view that 'the offence of seditious libel is now obsolete'. No one has cited Stephen on sedition as approvingly as Chief Justice Sinha did. The authoritative work, *Media Law: The Rights of Journalists and Broadcasters* by Geoffrey Robertson, QC, and Andrew Nicol, QC, opined that Stephen's definition of seditious libel 'is frighteningly broad and the crime has been used in the past to suppress radical political views. Even in the twentieth century it was used against an Indian nationalist and against Communist organisers. However, the post-war tendency has been to narrow the offence considerably. There has been no prosecution for sedition since 1947, and the offence now serves no purpose in the criminal law. In terms of Article 10, it is hard to see how it is necessary in a democratic society or proportionate to any legitimate aim.'

Sedition was indeed abolished in the UK through

the Coroners and Justice Act, 2009. The then justice minister, Claire Ward, said at the time of the Act's enactment: 'Sedition and seditious and defamatory libel are arcane offences from a bygone era when freedom of expression wasn't seen as the right it is today. Freedom of speech is now seen as the touchstone of democracy, and the ability of individuals to criticise the State is crucial to maintaining freedom.'

According to Claire Ward, 'The existence of these obsolete offences in this country had been used by other countries as justification for the retention of similar laws which have been actively used to suppress political dissent and restrict press freedom.' Perhaps she had India in mind.

Robertson and Nicol point out that 'many of the criminal laws that affect the media—official secrets and prevention of terrorism, and most of the laws relating to contempt, reporting restrictions and obscenity—cannot be invoked in the criminal courts by anyone except the Attorney-General or the Director of Public Prosecutions (who works under the Attorney's superintendence). In all these cases the Attorney-General is not bound to take legal action, even if the law has clearly been broken. He has a discretion—to prosecute or not to prosecute—

depending on his view of the public interest. In exercising his discretion he is entitled to take into account any consideration of public policy that bears on the issue—and the public policy in favour of free speech is important in deciding whether to launch official secrets or contempt or obscenity prosecution. Actions that appear to compromise free speech are likely to be criticised in Parliament, where the Attorney must answer for both his and the DPP's (Director of Public Prosecution) prosecution policy.'

Sir John Simon had said on 1 December 1925, in the House of Commons: 'There is no greater nonsense talked about the Attorney-General's duty than the suggestion that in all cases the Attorney-General ought to prosecute merely because he thinks there is what lawyers call "a case". It is not true, and no one who has held that office supposes that it is.' That is why both Sir Chimanlal Harilal Setalvad and Sir Ibrahim Rahimtullah advised the Governor of Bombay not to prosecute Gandhi for sedition. The result vindicated them. Gandhi emerged stronger after the trial. In the Kedar Nath case in 1962, as well as in later cases, the Supreme Court overlooked one fundamental difference between English law and Indian law. In England, the Attorney General's prior consent is necessary before a prosecution for sedition is launched. He acts in a quasi-judicial capacity, not as a party hack. In India, it is the central or even the state government that sanctions the prosecution (Section 196 of the Code of Criminal Procedure). Often, this executive act is performed for political, partisan and even communal reasons. One shocking case will suffice. All the documents are included in *Secular Horror: 15 Years Ordeal with Indian Secularism* by Mustafa Kamal Sherwani. The first information report for sedition was filed on 18 March 1985. The accused were acquitted on 25 July 2000—fifteen years later.

APPROPRIATING A JUDICIAL PREROGATIVE

No minister or executive officer has any right to pronounce on the guilt of a citizen, as Home Minister Rajnath Singh did on the occasion of the student protests in Jawaharlal Nehru University in February 2016. That right belongs to the courts. In a powerful dissent in *Gitlow vs New York* Justice Oliver Wendell Holmes, Jr. of the United States Supreme Court, gave a historic dissent with Justice Louis D. Brandeis's concurrence. Benjamin Gitlow, a member of the left wing of the Socialist Party, was convicted under the Criminal Anarchy Act for writing a pamphlet called *Left Wing Manifesto*, which advocated non-parliamentary methods. In 1925, the court affirmed his conviction. Holmes's dissent, in which Brandeis joined, said: 'It is said that this manifesto was more than a theory, that it was an incitement. Every idea is an incitement. It offers itself for belief and, if believed, it is acted on unless some other belief outweighs it or some failure of energy stifles the movement at its birth. The only difference between the expression of an opinion and an incitement in the narrower sense is the speaker's enthusiasm for the result. Eloquence may set fire to reason. But whatever may be thought of the redundant discourse before us, it had no chance of starting a present conflagration. If, in the long run, the beliefs expressed in proletarian dictatorship are destined to be accepted by the dominant forces of the community, the only meaning of free speech is that they should be given their chance to have their way.'

How much stronger then is the case for restraint when students' activities on a university campus are involved, as was the case in JNU? Involved here are two values: free speech and the autonomy of universities.

These are values that neither Rajnath Singh, the home minister, nor Smriti Irani, the human resource development minister, and least of all Amit Shah, the BJP's president, care for.

'Kings turn men into coins to which they assign what value they like, and which others are obliged to accept at the official rate, and not at their real worth.' François de La Rochefoucauld's maxim fits Amit Shah perfectly.

Shah behaves like a swadeshi Joseph McCarthy. His latest edict is that even organizing an event on Afzal Guru is anti-national. This is too late in the day. More to the point, it betrays his and the BJP's perverted concept of Indian nationalism and its pluralities. Many in the country, this writer included, have legitimate questions regarding Afzal Guru. These would include the following: Was an innocent man framed? Did he receive a fair trial? Was the Supreme Court's emotive approach the proper judicial way to proceed? In any liberal democracy, questions like these can be freely asked without incurring the kind of opprobrium and accusations that are increasingly becoming the norm in the country today.

If the nation cares for its values, it is time an organized campaign is launched against the law of sedition (which is sought to be saved by 'reforming' it) and BJP style McCarthyism ('anti-national'), and for the autonomy of universities.

We should take our cue, when it comes to laws governing our universities, from enlightened laws such as Section 43(1) of the British Education Act, 1986, which lays down: 'Every individual and body or persons concerned in the government of any establishment to which this section applies shall take such steps as are reasonably practicable to ensure that freedom of speech within the law is secured for members, students and employees of the establishment and for visiting speakers.' Such a statute will not be enacted in India, but we can and should unite against repressive laws and for the autonomy of universities.

II
THE ORIGINS OF 'BHARAT MATA KI JAI'

On 17 March 2016, the Rashtriya Swayamsevak Sangh (RSS) joint general secretary Dattatreya Hosabale declared that 'anyone who refused to say "Bharat Mata ki Jai" is anti-national for us'. Two days later, BJP President Amit Shah raised the pitch. He said that the BJP 'will not tolerate criticism of the country'.

He added, 'anti-national activity cannot be justified on the plea of freedom of expression'. Such irresponsible statements are unacceptable to citizens of any liberal democracy because no one has the right to prescribe what sort of statements and slogans are properly nationalistic and which aren't. No one has the right to take the law into his own hands, define the offence by himself and exert himself to express his refusal to 'tolerate' it. Even the state cannot wield executive power without the sanction of the law laid down by the legislature. I have written elsewhere that the Sangh Parivar's fondness for nationalism of this sort has to do with its agenda of forcing Hindu nationalism upon the country over Indian nationalism, but in this essay I will limit myself to why the right wing is so fond of the slogan 'Bharat Mata ki Jai'. Here are five reasons:

1. Wrote the BJP ideologue V. D. Savarkar in *Hindutva: Who is a Hindu:* 'Every stone here has a story of martyrdom to tell! Every inch of thy soil, O Mother! has been a sacrificial ground! Not only "where the Krishnasar is found" but from Kasmir to Sinhar it is "Land of sacrifice", sanctified with a Jnana Yajna or an Atmaajna (self-sacrifice). So to every Hindu, from the Santal to the Sadhu,

this Bharat bhumi this Sindhusthan is at once a Pitribhu and a Punyabhu—fatherland and a holy land.

'That is why in the case of some of our Mohammedan or Christian countrymen who had originally been forcibly converted to a non-Hindu religion and who consequently have inherited along with Hindus, a common Fatherland and a greater part of the wealth of a common culture— language, law, customs, folklore and history—are not and cannot be recognized as Hindus. For, though Hindusthan to them is Fatherland as to any other Hindu, yet it is not to them a Holyland too. Their holyland is far off in Arabia or Palestine. Their mythology and Godmen, ideas and heroes are not the children of this soil. Consequently their names and their outlook smack of a foreign origin...

'Ye, who by race, by blood, by culture, by nationality, possess almost all the essentials of Hindutva and had been forcibly snatched out of our ancestral home by the hand of violence— ye, have only to render wholehearted love to our common Mother and recognize her not only as Fatherland (Pitribhu) but even as a Holyland

(Punyabhu); and ye would be most welcome to the Hindu fold.' According to Savarkar, the country is an object of worship; 'a common Mother' who is also a Holyland.

2. RSS Supremo M. S. Golwalkar echoed the sentiment in the preface to his pamphlet *We or Our Nationhood Defined*, dated 22 March 1939. He wrote: 'I offer this work to the public as an [*sic*] humble offering at the holy feet of the Divine Mother—the Hindu Nation in the hope that She will graciously accept this worship from an undeserving child of Her Own.' The 'Hindu Nation' is approximated to the 'common Mother' and both are objects of worship.

3. Chetan Bhatt of Goldsmiths College, University of London, has written a very incisive and well-documented analysis, *Hindu Nationalism: Origins, Ideologies and Modern Myths*. He points out that the song 'Vande Mataram' is a 'virtual anthem for the contemporary Hindutva movement'. It means 'Hail to Thee, O Mother (land)' and figures in Bankim Chandra Chatterjee's novel *Anandamath*. Chetan Bhatt characterizes the slogan Bharat Mata ki Jai (Victory to (Holy) Mother Land) as the 'Hinduized nationalist slogan'.

He recalls that 'during the 1991 election, the BJP had campaigned on the slogan "Towards Ram Rajya". Its election manifesto declared it to be "the party of Nationalism, Holism and Integral Humanism" and exactly reproduced Savarkar's definition of Hindutva: "From the Himalayas to Kanya Kumari, this country has always been one. We have had many States, but we were always one people. We always looked upon our country as Matribhoomi, Punyabhoomi (Motherland and Holyland)."'

In a brilliant passage, Bhatt writes: 'Of considerable significance is that a strategy involving devotion was used, rather than the more austere paths of esoteric knowledge or physical practice that exist in (especially upper) caste Hinduism. This required the formulation of novel, overarching nationalist religious symbols, which cannot be said to have traditional endorsements within Hinduism, but which could nevertheless not be explicitly opposed either. One key symbol was that of Bharat Mata, a devotional rendering of the Mother Goddess as equivalent to the geographical territory of "Akhand Bharat". In the Hindutva symbolic imaginary 'Bharat Mata' stands in for 'Hindu Rashtra', and worship of the latter.

4. B. R. Purohit's able work *Hindu Revivalism and Indian Nationalism* further explains the true significance of Bankim Chandra Chatterjee's novel *Anandamath*. 'Durga, the goddess and the mother became one with the country, the greater goddess and the mother. In his well-known novel, *Anandamath*, he presented the country as Goddess Kali, black because of intense misery, naked because denuded of wealth, with human skulls round her neck because the country was no less than a vast burial ground. But the future India would be like radiant Durga who will annihilate the "demons" and usher in an era of plenty and prosperity.'

Chatterjee resorts to similar imagery in 'Vande Mataram' that some regard as an unofficial national anthem. 'I bow to Thee, goddess of wealth, pure and peerless, richly-watered, richly fruited, the Mother! I bow to Thee Mother dark-hued, candid, sweetly smiling, jewelled and adorned, the holder of wealth, the lady of plenty, the Mother!' Thus nationalism, with Bankim Chandra, became the national religion.

Purohit adds: 'Bankim Chandra Chatterjee raised

nationalism to the dignity of a religion. He stirred
the souls of many men in this country by placing
new religious ideals before them. The country did
not remain with him a mere fact of geography.
He identified the motherland with old religious
deities. He added a new image—the image of the
"Motherland"—in the pantheon of the Hindus.
The "Vande Mataram" song became an equally
inspiring national hymn. In doing so, he promoted
the spirit of nationalism'.

Writing in the *Indian Express* in 1998, the political
commentator Yogesh Vajpeyi had this to say:
'Bankim…gave the project to unite Hindus under
one umbrella a mass appeal. His eulogy of goddess
Kali in the hymn "Vande Mataram" instilled the
idea of the motherland as a divine entity.'

5. Finally, we would do well to remember that the
oath prescribed by the Rashtriya Swayamsevak
Sangh for its men goes as follows, 'Remembering
Almighty God and my forebears, I take this
oath. For the betterment of my sacred Hindu
religion, Hindu culture, and Hindu community,
I will devote myself to the prosperity of my
Holy Motherland. I swear that I shall serve the
Rashtriya Swayamsevak Sangh with my body, my

mind, and my money. I will be faithful to this oath throughout my life.'

This is the record on 'Bharat Mata'. When the upstarts of the BJP tell us that it is 'anti-national' not to proclaim it, it is because they do not bear loyalty to Indian nationalism, but to Hindu nationalism or Hindutva. Purohit writes in *Hindu Revivalism and Indian Nationalism* about the evolution of Hindu nationalism and Indian nationalism and how the two differ: 'The two nationalisms—the Hindu and the Indian—were fundamentally in opposition to each other with respect to their ideals. The former was exclusive, narrowly based, mixed with religion and partial: it considered the Hindus the only nationals of Hindustan and did not include other communities living in India within its scope; it had grown even militant and aggressive towards other religions. The latter believed in a composite culture of India, and viewed India as a nation composed of all the communities living therein. It was broad based, pacifist, secular, democratic and liberal in temperament. One exalted a community over other communities while the other emphasised unity in the diversity of various communities. The one had great belief in centralised leadership and in militancy; the other was wedded to liberal and democratic traditions...'

To preserve the ideals that have been bequeathed to us by our founding fathers, and to ensure that the liberal, democratic traditions of this country continue to flourish, we should be very clear that the only nationalism that deserves our support is Indian nationalism. That is something we should never forget.

FROM
NATIONAL
CULTURE TO
CULTURAL
NATIONALISM

——

SADANAND MENON

Over two decades ago, I was present at an unusually crowded press conference in Delhi. Unusual because it was to launch the India tour of the celebrated international dancer/choreographer Pina Bausch. The Indian media hardly ever grants more than cursory attention to artists, and here were over a hundred journalists crowding into the Azad Bhavan auditorium of the ICCR. The press conference was being conducted by Dr Georg Lechner, the then head of the Goethe-Institut. From the outset, Lechner was trying to get Pina to concede the 'German-ness' of her work. Pina would inhale from her cigarette, blow a couple of smoke rings and say, 'No. No!' A second time, too, she evaded the question. The third time when he said, 'Come on, Pina, admit it, at bottom you are a German artist', Pina looked him straight in the eye and said, 'Georg, had I been a bird, would you have called me a German bird?' The audience applauded spontaneously.

This is a question all of us need to reflect on deeply—our own self-implication in our respective nationalisms.

I

Rabindranath Tagore was categorical about his position on nationalism as a 'menace' in the prolonged debates over it in his novel *Gora* (1910) as well as in his essays like 'East and West' or 'Swadeshi Samaj'. In *Nationalism*, first published in 1917, he goes as far as to say 'The nation is the greatest evil', and states 'it is my conviction that my countrymen will gain truly their India by fighting against that education which teaches them that a country is greater than the ideals of humanity'. A couple of decades later, Tagore again cautioned against rabid nationalism at a time when multiple imaginaries of nationhood were floating around in pre-Independence India: there was the idea of the Hindu Rashtra that Bankim Chandra Chatterjee had given birth to in his *Anandamath*, to be elaborated later by V. D. Savarkar; a clearly articulated idea of an Islamic state too was afloat; a Khalistan had already been proposed; down south, the movement for an independent Dravidasthan was in full swing; Dr B. R. Ambedkar had mooted the concept of a separate Dalitstan. It was into this assortment of nationalist imaginaries that Tagore edged in his proposition that a nation can be both mrinmaya (territorial) as well as chinmaya (ideational). So when Pina Bausch claims the artistic prerogative to override nationality and locate herself in a universal space of the aesthetic commons she sounds very Tagorean.

II

The late U. R. Ananthamurthy used to narrate his experience with the compelling pull of national identity. Once, in London, someone asked him who he was, and he said, 'I'm an Indian.' Later, he reflected on it. Why did I say that, I'm no rabid flag-waving patriot; what made me give that answer! A few days later, he was in Delhi, where someone asked him who he was, and he said, 'I'm a Kannadiga'. Again, he interrogated himself. I'm no Kannada language chauvinist, what made me respond in that manner! A little later, in Bengaluru, someone asked him who he was, and he said 'I'm from Thirthahalli.' Again, he was troubled. I'm no nativist or back-to-the-roots agitator, then what made me give such a reply! And then, as his story went, some days later he was in Thirthahalli where no one asked him who he was because everyone there knew him. But Ananthamurthy used to narrate this story to describe the call of a subliminal national, regional, local identity that permeates our subconscious and can be roused at will for good or for bad. Somewhat in the way Albert Camus used the metaphor of the plague bacillus being roused periodically for the edification of mankind.

III

Incipient, amorphous, contradictory and always-in-formation, national consciousness or nationalism precedes the emergence of all nations.

This constructs itself around two visible axes—the political and the cultural. While the political engages with concepts of freedom, self-determination, sovereignty and self-reliance, the cultural tosses up difficult, contentious paradigms of identity, a coherent historical past, artistic heritage and a moral self.

As the consciousness of a nation-in-the-making accelerates, the idea of a national culture begins to consolidate, becoming the visible face of nationalism.

Culture and nationalism have ever been close allies. Culture has always set up the contours for national movements and nations have used culture as a convenient flag to wave in ideas of superiority or exclusivity. They constantly service each other in the project of manufacturing identities and consolidating boundaries—real and imaginary.

This lasts well into the formation of the nation. But, quite independent of this and not always lurking in the shadows, we also witness the parallel articulation of a rabid, virulent idea of cultural nationalism, which strives to define the political nation in narrow, restrictive and culturally monolithic and exclusionary terms.

A nation that, at some point, lets its political primacy be eroded and overrun by cultural nationalism can be construed to be on the verge of an implosion. India is today on the edge of such an implosion. Majoritarian nationalism masquerading as a 'cultural good' is systematically displacing the urgent imperatives of the political economy from the driver's seat, and is pushing the nation onto a path entirely contradictory to what it strived for or claimed during its movement for national independence.

What is visible today is a new hatred for the idea of democracy as we know it and for the rights as guaranteed in the Constitution. This is quite in keeping with the agenda of cultural nationalism, which strives—through generating a climate of intolerance and intimidation—to keep civil society in a state of constant agitation by subjecting it to constant attack.

IV

Cultural nationalism, by any definition, is a rogue version of nationalism which is already present in concepts of the nation state. Its cunning agenda is to evacuate all ideas of political rights from the idea of a nation state and transplant in its place ideas of cultural rights, obviously weighted in favour of concepts of primogeniture, racial purity and genetic ancestry as contained in ideas like janmabhumi or birthland/homeland and other emotive aspects that touch upon shared language, food and consanguinity. It is a highly charged area of irrational self-beliefs that give little credence to claims of history or any other kind of scientific research. It is an imaginary homeland constructed out of imaginary hurts, insults, wounds and defeats inflicted by imaginary enemies, who always belong to religions and regions not (you believe, are) your own. It is a strange, anxious individual who will not pay the slightest heed to one's own proven hybridity. In history, nothing stays 'pure'. Or, as Salman Rushdie would have it, it's all subject to 'mongrelization'.

In the Indian context, the RSS's effort has been to construct a 'national identity' which is anterior to and elides over the colonial as well Islamic periods of recent times to reach out to an 'authentic' India of the hoary past, which remains emblematic of its 'real' culture— unique, untrammelled and unadulterated by colonial or Islamic hybridity. In the past, this version found favour with the reigning tenets of Orientalist thought which divided the world into neat, essentialized compartments of the 'East' and the 'West'. The East was, then, nothing but 'spiritual'. Partha Chatterjee, in *Nationalist Thought and the Colonial World: A Derivative Discourse*, has clearly argued how these tropes play out, sometimes straight and sometimes inverting their own claims.

A constant character of the manufacture of cultural nationalism, therefore, is the constant and nagging 'unhappiness' over the narratives of the past which digress from specious claims of purity, undifferentiated unity and political power. Every attempt then is to exhibit unbridled triumphalism over its own antiquity and past glories that anticipate similar fortunes in the future.

V

Soon after the NDA came to power in 1998 under

Atal Bihari Vajpayee, an extraordinary event happened at the National Museum, Delhi. The Harappan Gallery in the museum was quickly 'renovated'. As you entered that section, space had been created on the left wall of the gallery to inscribe a 'civilizational timeline'. So there were Sumerian and Assyrian and Babylonian and Egyptian civilizations, all indicated through coloured bands of varying lengths as per their historic antiquity—from 1200 BCE to 2500 BCE. There were about ten or twelve bands in different colours and of diverse lengths. The Chinese civilization, which originated in 3200 BCE, was indicated by a long red band which went halfway across the wall. Above this was a saffron band proudly proclaiming 'Indian Civilization 7000 BCE', which went all the way across the wall, dwarfing every other band. The figure, which is a figment of the imagination, has been floating around in the Indian national consciousness since the time Bal Gangadhar Tilak, in his essay 'The Arctic Home in the Vedas', had somehow configured the Vedic period to be of around that antiquity. Sometimes these inflated figures were useful during the anti-colonial movement to mobilize nationalist opinion and to thumb your nose at the colonialist. However, post-Independence, even as these figures and strategies get contested through more rigorous research, they do get commandeered for purposes that aid in creating a majoritarian version of historic exceptionalism.

This is on par with what Amartya Sen has claimed in *The Argumentative Indian* about how the BJP has been consistently working towards popularizing the Hindutva theory through misrepresenting historic facts, fabricating evidence, inventing origin stories from popular mythologies and using violence and force on moderate Hindus as well as other minorities. To project India as a Hindu country and reclaim it exclusively for Hindus, it has rewritten Indian history as essentially a history of Hindu civilization, and sees it as an essential prerequisite for establishing a grand Hindu vision of India.

VI

In this essay, I intend to touch upon five aspects pertaining to the phenomenon of cultural nationalism and, through them, trace the contours of its development, consolidation and possible future. The five aspects that seem to me important to examine are cultural nationalism's engagement with the past, with politics, with issues of gender, with constructions of culture and with its fascination with violence. Of course, most of these themes will overlap and criss-cross each other, which merely points to the complex web of physical and psychological networks that cultural nationalism sets up and which we encounter in our everyday life as being 'normative', until we put each one of them to the rigorous test of close, unsentimental scrutiny.

VII

Ideas of cultural nationalism emerged hand in hand with late nineteenth-century ideas of nationhood itself. Nationalist leaders like Tilak worked on constructing the idea of a glorious and ancient Indian past, heavily inflected with Hindu symbology, as a strategy to fight the imperialist. This was one of the ways in which the national movement hoped to forge a common Indian identity based on a glorious past (composed in equal parts of myth, legend and select incorporations of historical facts). The idea of the past that the national struggle sought to create in its early days was one of a pre-historic India of mythic origins that was divine, pure, monolithic and untainted by any polluting 'external' influence. This itself was a myth, for the subcontinent has been host to an unending procession of cultures and claimants who have tromped through it over at least three millennia. Yet the attempt was to make culture the sole base for the formation of the independent nation. Inevitably, because of the majoritarian Hindu population and the national leadership that represented them, this notion of the past that was more or less upper caste and Hindu became conflated and interchangeable with the idea of the new emerging nation in the minds of most of those involved in the independence movement. In some cases, this was deliberate, in others it was inadvertent. The prototype of how cultural nationalism came to be constructed here can be divided into a few distinct phases.

The first phase is what would be best described as incipient nationalism. It begins with the early impulse to shape the country's cultural identity by reforming Hinduism itself. English educated, upper-class/caste Indians of the period begin to take to heart the critique as well as construction of Hindu society by 'well-meaning' Western scholars. Customs considered 'barbaric' like child marriages, the practice of sati, the isolation of widows, the dedication of women to temples as 'devadasis', caste discrimination are all seen as retrograde and deplorable. Reformists like Raja Ram Mohan Roy emerge in the early part of the nineteenth century to campaign actively against such 'evils' and set the house in order. The setting up of the Brahmo Samaj is clearly an early step in articulating a self-conscious new nationalism. It gets further articulated by more aggressive reformers later in the century like Ishwar Chandra Vidyasagar and Jyotiba Phule. Swami Dayanand Saraswati sets up the Arya Samaj, which simultaneously calls for reform within the Hindu religion and builds defences against erosion by other religions through elaborate rituals of purity and restitution. The frenzied 'ghar wapsi' of today is not all that original an idea. Here the Vedas are considered to be the foundation of Indian nationalism. Hindu tradition is invoked for claiming cultural autonomy, for critiquing certain social practices, as well as for providing cultural foundations for assertive nationalism. Mohinder Singh, in 'Crisis & Critique: Diagnosis of the Present in Nationalist Discourse in Hindi, 1870–1908', has made the point that 'nationalism absorbs traditions superficially; in truth it remains nationalism's suppressed other'.

As A. G. Noorani points out in his essay on the origins of Bharat Mata, a more militant version of nationalism is provided in 1882 by the publication of the novel *Anandamath* by Bankim Chandra Chatterjee. This was to soon assume the proportion of a manifesto for Hindu nationalism, as Bankim plays with all the tropes of exclusive nationalism— protecting his nation from any external defilement. His idealized nation is Anandamath. The deity he worships is an already militarized, ready-for-battle Krishna who will lead his chosen ones to victory. And, of course, 'Vande Mataram' is the battle cry around which he rouses the hordes. It is pertinent here to evoke Sudipta Kaviraj's masterly study, *The Unhappy Consciousness: Bankim Chandra Chattopadhyay and the Formation of Nationalist Discourse in India*, where he suggests how Bankim works around the fantasy of war against 'outsiders', which included the British and the Muslims. He thus provides a powerful imagery for a future nationalism, which was influential enough to be celebrated in theatre and cinema over the next seventy years. And 'Vande Mataram' itself (coupled with 'Bharat Mata ki Jai') emerged as the new talisman with which to measure not only one's patriotism but one's very nationality. The sheer ecstasy and rapture into which Hindutva hacks went when A. R. Rahman performed in a virtuoso track of 'Vande Mataram' nearly a decade ago was never repeated for any of his other works.

In 1905, coinciding with the partition of Bengal, Abanindranath Tagore paints an image of 'Banga Mata' (Mother Bengal). This was soon to be recast as 'Bharat Mata' (Mother India), which marked one of the earliest attempts, building on those by Bankim, to cast the nation in the shape of a benevolent mother. This was still a benign image in the gentle wash style of the Bengal School, where the image is soft and radiant and holds promise of bounty, prosperity and benevolence. Subsequently, as the struggle for independence intensified, so did this image of the benevolent mother become increasingly ferocious, a cross between a Durga and a Kali, riding a tiger and fully armed. Bharat Mata took on a distinctly militant identity that was used to mobilize the Hindu flock, irrespective of political persuasion.

It must be said here that 'Bharat Mata ki Jai' is not an attribute of patriotism, but of deep patriarchy. Extreme mother-love is a camouflage for extreme misogyny. Over the past few years in India, the nature of the violence inflicted on women during rapes, riots and caste retributions is of an order seldom witnessed before in any part of the world, except perhaps, in

Bosnia during the civil war, or in the Congo, or in Sri Lanka during the final moments of the pogrom against the civilian Tamil population there. From the barbarity of the jawans of the Assam Rifles on Manorama Devi, to incessant mass rapes by soldiers in Kashmir, to the graphic and horrific brutalities (that were videotaped) on even pregnant women in Gujarat in 2002, to the Nirbhaya case in Delhi, there is no evidence to prove that devotion towards an abstract 'Bharat Mata' translates into even a semblance of affection or respect for real flesh-and-blood women. Indeed, here it is only literally the flesh and blood that seems to matter. Add to this the kind of vile trolling and rank verbal and mental abuse that independent women activists/writers who stand up for rights and against bullying—like, say, Kavita Krishnan, Teesta Setalvad, Arundhati Roy, Shabnam Hashmi, Shehla Rashid, Rana Ayyub and others—are attacked with indicates a level of morbidity and sexual repression that should be unsustainable in a democracy. Cultural nationalism can truly be said to have arrived when this confusion about one's identity and sexuality produces a permanent pathology of inadequacy, about which Austrian psychoanalyst Wilhelm Reich has so insightfully written in *The Mass Psychology of Fascism*

(1993). For Reich, cultural nationalism is the basic emotional attitude of the suppressed man. He sees the 'authoritarian family' as the base of the middle classes, which is held together with the help of religious fears and rampant mysticism, infused in turn by sexual guilt embedded in their emotions. Religion, thus, leads to negation of sexual desire. Sexual disability results in lowering of self-confidence.

This is often compensated by the 'brutalization of sexuality'. The good doctor was analysing Germany of the 1930s; he might as well have been putting contemporary India on the couch.

VIII

The quest for a coherent 'national culture' during the various phases of a national movement creates many aberrations that last well into the post-colonial state. That extraordinary philosopher of anti-colonialism, Frantz Fanon, has made abundantly clear that, 'A national culture under colonial domination is a contested culture whose destruction is sought in systematic fashion.' Yet, he warns against the pitfalls of such national consciousness which, he says, 'instead of being the all-embracing crystallisation of the innermost hopes of the whole people, instead of being the immediate and most obvious result of the mobilization of the people, will be in any case only an empty shell, a crude and fragile travesty of what it might have been'. It sets up many a mock battle internally which later goes on to become a vehicle for mutant forms of cultural nationalism. Often, the agency for this is the idea of the 'moral nation'.

The national movement sets up its legitimacy vis-à-vis the colonial apparatus as a morally superior idea that is jettisoning all its old ambiguities and re-inventing itself. Such an image is, primarily, a moral construction, which admits no 'pollutant'.

Take the case of Bharatanatyam and how it was adapted in the late 1920s/early 1930s from its earlier version as Sadirattam or Dasiattam, performed by the socially ostracized community of devadasis (belonging to the Isai Vellalar caste). It was one of those elements of culture that was aggressively appropriated and transformed to fit an imagined, idealized Hindu upper-caste cultural identity. When the original dance form that unabashedly portrayed eroticism and conveyed sensuality (shringara) transited to the upper class/caste Brahmin community in cosmopolitan Madras, it also resulted in a bowdlerizing and sanitizing of the form.

Often we find that dance forms originating in subaltern classes or non-dominant communities present a trajectory of upward mobility during specific phases of nation-building, during which these forms are fumigated, deodorized, gentrified and de-eroticized. During such clinical de-sexualization and domestication of the forms as they cross class/caste boundaries we also find a distinct transformation in body-usage, as the erotic charge is sublimated within false religiosity.

In the case of Bharatanatyam, this led to the rather swift conversion of the dance form into a platform for entirely mythologized and socially sanctified content, almost transforming it into a vehicle for proselytization. A distinctly Brahminical content for the dance gained currency as the project for restructuring collective memory was initiated at the height of the national movement. While myth and memory conventionally serve to preserve identity and provoke bonding through the evocation of a shared cultural heritage, these can also be used as political weapons to impose a hegemonic memorial narrative that seeks to privilege a narrow vision of specific historical events.

Bharatanatyam is one among a few cultural objects

today, like the Ganesh Utsav or Raksha Bandhan or the thickening sindoor that women across communities display or freshly minted greetings like 'Jai Shri Krishna' or the bhajan sandhyas which are being deployed on the side of majoritarian cultural nationalism.

IX

The aggressive turn towards cultural nationalism we are witnessing today with assaults on members of minority religions and Dalits; growing harassment of those with different racial features, like Indian citizens from the northeastern regions or foreign nationals from African countries; the rather heavy dose of ultra-nationalism that is being pumped up to demonize students in JNU or CUH; the assaults on journalists and civil rights activists in Chhattisgarh; the vilification of scholars like Jean Drèze or Kancha Ilaiah or Nivedita Menon—none of these can be seen as merely contemporary phenomena. These are tendencies and impulses of self-righteousness and aggressive nationalism that have been incubated right from the earliest days of the national movement. Many of these tendencies had stayed underground and hibernated until the soil and temperature were ripe for them to sprout. Many others stayed invisible because no one was paying attention, because they seemed marginal and were tolerated.

One could, perhaps, speculate that some of this at least could have been checked and countered if the considerably large Left and secular forces, which believed in cultural freedom, individual freedom and creativity had better opposed the incessant romanticization of the past, and the constantly parroted notions of Hindu culture being the basis of Indian culture. In the 1940s, leftist organizations like the Progressive Writers' Association and the Indian People's Theatre Association (IPTA) did put up a credible front against such narrow nationalist projections through their considerable work in literature, theatre, cinema and engaged resistance in the field. Their countervailing narrative of humanity and universalism to that of the exclusionary and violent narrative of the Hindu Right did make a considerable difference. But in the past several decades the Left has been unable to sustain this and even seemed disinterested in engaging with ideas of nationhood, nationalism, religion, culture and identities. It has proved ineffective in checking the rise of aggressive Hindu notions of cultural nationalism. The same could be said of the liberals, too, who even as they saw the manifestations of cultural nationalism, dismissed it as a loony fringe, with little effort to challenge or counter it.

As a political force, cultural nationalism draws heavily upon the past to shape the identity of the present. It is up to the democratic forces to question the authenticity of such constructs and expose their majoritarian and hegemonic underpinnings. Wherever this political argument does not take root, cultural nationalism marches in with its triumphal banners.

X

The creation, evolution and maintenance of a national culture is at base a political act, and is intended to serve political ends. A key component of the politics of cultural nationalism resides in its ability to create an enemy. This enables the idea to be sold to and accepted by a large number of people and enables the proponents of the concept to manufacture threats and crises at will. The idea of the enemy changes from time to time, but in India the long-term project of Hindu cultural nationalism has always constructed the Muslim as the 'enemy', the 'Other', who the forces of nationalism have to be vigilant about and keep in check. Their loyalties were always questioned and their motives always suspect. The recent case of the attack on Kashmiri students because they chose to applaud the winning West Indies side in the T-20 World Cup is a case in point.

Even those leaders who defended at every opportunity the fact that India was a multi-cultural, multi-religious, liberal nation, inadvertently contributed to the building of the idea of the national culture as essentially Hindu. One such example can be sourced to Mahatma Gandhi's 'Hind Swaraj' or 'Self-Rule'. By this, Gandhiji did not only mean freedom from the colonial ruler, he also meant the need to transform oneself, to look within and take control of one's life and destiny. His emphasis of the Vedantic concept of atmabal or soul-force in order to achieve this transformation inadvertently contributed to the advancing of Hindu nationalist ideas. Even though in the recent book *Hindutva or Hind Swaraj* U. R. Ananthamurthy proposes that V. D. Savarkar's ideas in *Hindutva* have an antidote in Gandhi's vision as elaborated in *Hind Swaraj*, he does not point out that both these politico-cultural propositions spring from the same fount of a yearning for a nostalgic past and taking strength from there for transforming the present. No wonder Ananthamurthy laments the fact that, in this argument, Savarkar's muscular idea of the past seems to have won, while Gandhi's softer and more accommodative idea seems to have lost.

These early attempts by Hindu nationalists and others to construct a heavily Hindu inflected national identity met with little or no resistance. The only major national leader who unequivocally challenged these ideas of nationalism was Rabindranath Tagore, who thought there was the possibility of a deep malevolence that might be lurking within our love for our nation and who felt nationalism was a threat to liberal societies where caste and other issues divided the people.

Partition provided a further fillip to the idea of Hindu cultural nationalism, which in the eyes of large sections of the population was now inseparable from Indian cultural nationalism or Indian national culture. Pakistan became the 'Other', and Indian Muslims became a subset of this 'Other'.

Over the years, successive governments began to show signs of subtle transformation. From being instruments of law-giving and governance, they gradually transformed into instruments in the service of right-wing nationalism while paying lip service to constitutional ideas of liberty, fraternity and equality.

Today, the reason the RSS (and its affiliates) is in the ascendant is because of its long and patient work in constructing a national identity in its image. Conditions for its further expansion are ideal. The forces of those who could oppose its spread are in disarray, a sizeable proportion of the middle class who are not vocal supporters of Hindutva are either passive or distracted by promises of economic betterment, and the less privileged have become, as a result of decades of cultivation by the right wing, foot soldiers of Hindutva. As a result of all these factors, illusory threats like those of conversion, cultural pollution, insults to some idea of pure Indian culture and so on are used to further build up the threat of the 'Other'. It is immaterial to the right wing that this cynical exploitation of the majority community will not improve the quality of their lives or magically create the superpower of their dreams. All that these assiduous creators of pseudo-Indian culture are interested in, for the most part, is the furthering of their own political power.

XI

One of the most modern ideas about women to be

had from anywhere in the world is the pre-Hindu concept of Sakambhari (first seen in an Indus Valley seal) or the autonomous woman who is self-generative, independent, complete unto herself and from whose body nature and vegetation spring. So too the idea of the Salabhanjika (Gandhara sculptures, Mathura), the woman who is coterminous with nature and prosperity. Similar ideas about women can be found in early sculptural representations from Sanchi to Aihole to Konark. This was the place Indian women had in pre-patriarchal times.

The cultural nationalism project of Hindutva will have nothing to do with that kind of an open 'past'. This is unsurprising because, without exception, communal nationalisms take the male point of view and attempt to feminize the nation state into the Motherland or, in our case, Bharat Mata. Along with this come idealized notions of racial and ethnic/caste purity. The woman becomes the carrier of this cultural burden. She is expected to be chaste and virtuous. She should be protected from the gaze and attacks of the 'Other'.

At the moment, what we are seeing play out is the ongoing clash between the ideas and practice of feminism and right-wing notions of what Indian women should be. Short skirts, the celebration of Valentine's Day, inter-caste marriages, inter-religious romance, women in the workplace, LGBT issues, to name just a few, are anathema to the Sangh Parivar. For, if the image of the idealized woman is broken, out with it go notions of the family (as conceived in the mind of the right wing) as a microcosm of the state, with the role of women being limited to being mothers and those who keep the family together. Ironically, some of the most popular forms of TV and movie entertainment glorify ideas of women propagated by the Sangh Parivar, although these forms of entertainment are not necessarily sanctioned or funded by right-wing organizations. What will be the outcome of this battle between right wing notions of women, and the demand of growing members of twenty-first-century Indian women to be liberated and autonomous? If one looks to the evolution of open, liberal societies around the world in which women eventually managed to break the shackles of patriarchal, conservative ideologies, it would seem that Indian women will eventually regain the idea of the Sakambhari—the idea of free, autonomous woman. My friend and mentor, dancer/choreographer Chandralekha, missed no opportunity in each of her ten productions, to evoke and assert the idea of such women who are swadheena vallabha—free and subservient to none—as a permanent strategy of speaking back to Hindutva in a deeper conceptual language that it is scared of.

XII

On the day the Babri Masjid was pulled down, 6 December 1992, forty cameramen were attacked by the mob of RSS/VHP rioters. Most of them lost their cameras and films, only a few managed to flee to Delhi with visual evidence of the destruction. I had described this large-scale destruction of visual evidence then as 'the blinding of the nation'. Since then, the threat from the street to fundamental freedoms of speech, creativity and culture has ballooned now to epidemic proportions. In times past, on occasion, the threat to artistic freedom came from the state, now, as a result of decades of indoctrination and administrative collusion, the violence comes from the street.

From the 1990s onwards, street thugs and rioters have threatened, beaten, maimed and assassinated writers, artists, journalists, university professors—anyone, in short, who has dared express themselves in any way that does not conform to what has received their sanction. We now serially name Narendra Dabholkar, Govind Pansare and Malleshappa Kalburgi as martyrs to the cause of free thought and free speech. But this list, unfortunately, is likely to swell as the genie of violence has been released from the bottle. The kind of unchecked expression of hatred in public space from the apparatchiks of the Hindutva brigade that we have heard expressed against JNU students like Kanhaiya Kumar, Umar Khalid and Anirban Bhattacharya is a window to the deeply disturbed mind of the nation. French public intellectual Jean-Paul Sartre, in his provocative preface to Fanon's *The Wretched of the Earth*, wrote, 'In other days France was the name of a country. We should take care that in 1961 it does not become the name of a nervous disease.' There is a lesson in it for contemporary India.

It is no coincidence that this is the period that has seen the rise to power of the Sangh Parivar, both in the political sphere as well as in large parts of civil society. While there have been instances of attacks on writers and journalists during the reign of Congress and other governments, it is indisputable that they have reached their apogee when the Hindu right wing has been in power. The hydra heads of the RSS and its affiliates are on the permanent lookout for social and cultural spaces to aggrandize.

What this has succeeded in doing is create an atmosphere of permanent suspicion that surrounds any artistic or creative endeavour. When writers, journalists, poets and painters are constantly looking over their shoulder at real or imagined threats, their creative output cannot but suffer. And the state instead of providing reassurance amplifies the threat, as when the Culture Minister Mahesh Sharma, a man whose cultural credentials are risible, made the extraordinary suggestion that 'if [writers] are unable to write, let them first stop writing'.

In this steadily worsening atmosphere, there was one ray of positive action. Towards the end of 2015, in an unprecedented show of solidarity, dozens of writers/artists/scientists returned awards bestowed on them by the state to protest the stifling of their freedom to create. In Vadodara, the Gujarati poet Anil Joshi, a 1990 Sahitya Akademi awardee, said, 'The atmosphere has become hateful. There is no breathing space and no freedom of expression for literary writers. It is like losing oxygen because we are writers who wish for free breathing space. I do not need an oxygen cylinder in the form of awards to live. The attack on the writers is unfortunate and has taken away the freedom of expression.'

Kashmiri writer Ghulam Nabi Khayal said, 'What is happening in India pains me. To return an award is the only way to express my resentment...'

As expected, the government's response was less than satisfactory.

A noteworthy feature of the response of the Narendra Modi government and organizations of the Sangh Parivar to the relentless attacks on freedom of expression has been their combativeness against suggestions that they are tampering with fundamental rights. In times past, they may have managed expressions of contrition, but now senior spokespersons of the government like Smriti Irani and Sharma openly attack those who stand up for their rights.

All of this is very much in keeping with the project started in the early decades of the twentieth century by votaries of Hindutva like Savarkar and Golwalkar to create a uniform, monolithic culture that conformed to their own ideals. What is worrying now is the enthusiastic resort to violence in a desperate attempt to fit the ideology onto the social base. In a country as big and old as India, with tens of thousands of cultural influences acting upon and inspiring its writers, intellectuals, journalists and others (who in turn will generate a myriad non-conformist cultural creations and influences), it is unlikely the Hindutva project will succeed in the long term. But, obviously, forces opposed to such grand agendas of majoritarian fascism need to pool together resources—either from electoral politics, or from the intellectual sphere, or through cultural activism—to create multiple platforms that are innovative, stubborn and courageous and that can dismantle such narrow ideologies. Ideally, the attempt to roll back the commandeering of Indian culture by the right wing should have started in earnest a few decades ago, but most liberals and intellectuals believed nothing would go wrong and that Indian society would be more resilient to such assaults. They couldn't have been more mistaken. In fact, the social base in India at the moment, particularly of the rapidly expanding middle class, is a demonstrably reactionary base. The attempts to manipulate aspects of Indian culture would not succeed if there weren't sizeable numbers of the Hindu majority who didn't support it. But there are equally sizeable numbers who are indifferent to the agenda of the Hindu Right if not actively opposed to it. It is important that all those who cherish the considerable breathing space that our

Constitution affords us realize that the only way to prevent it from being totally hijacked is by coming together and standing up to be counted. The writers who returned their awards were in the vanguard of the battle. Obviously, this can only be the beginning.

XIII

Heightened violence from the street (aimed at anyone who strayed from the right-wing norm of cultural nationalism) began to increase after the demolition of the Babri Masjid and became an administrative style during the first BJP-led ministry from 1998-2003. However, subsequent to the BJP's return to power at the centre with an absolute majority in 2014, two further trends became discernible. The first was the massive upswing in the influence of social media trolls who attacked any who dared censure Modi and other members of the Sangh Parivar, and the second was that the government itself began to participate in attacks on anyone who had the temerity to criticize it or the majoritarian agenda. From 2014 there is a noticeable shrinking of public spaces from where opposition can be mounted against the blatantly aggressive posturing and actions of members of the Sangh Parivar. In the past it was often such public opinion that served to regulate and moderate extremist politics. Of course, cultural aggression is not the prerogative of the Sanghis alone. Elsewhere in the country, too, the sense of intolerance has been on the rise with administrations controlled by parties like Mamata Banerjee's TMC or J. Jayalalithaa's AIADMK behaving like the BJP's B-team and unleashing the cops and the mobs at the slightest sign of disaffection towards right-wing politics. British India used its sedition laws with restraint and chose worthy opponents. Free India uses the same sedition laws so freely that we now have the anomaly of a sizeable section of citizens who are both seditious and anti-national without even realizing it. There is a distinct possibility that in the near future we might enter the Guinness Book of Records as a unique nation of anti-nationals.

XIV

One of the reasons for the unchecked rise of cultural nationalism over the past many decades and its easy visibility and belligerence in public and institutional spaces is, I believe, the almost seven decades of indifference and the throttling of the 'public sphere' in India. It has led to a condition that Noam Chomsky has defined as the 'democratic deficit'. It is Chomsky's term for describing the fatal inability of state institutions to contribute positively towards sustaining democratic principles; indeed, these systems perform the opposite function by choking information, dialogue, dissent and the crucial sharing of opinion. The day-to-day engagements, so necessary to create a functioning democratic culture within which the public can play a role in determining policies, is effectively throttled.

The emergence of 'public sphere' as a notional device—during the long passage from a monarchical to a more open, democratic form of society—imagined it as a level playing field for plural and contesting interests to enter into dialogue and, as posited by scholars of the Frankfurt School, extend the formal limits of democracy.

Within the binary counterposing of 'state' and 'society', the 'public sphere' found legitimization as a site for contested public opinion, which would provide the check-and-balance against any arbitrary exercise of the state's authority or a deviation from any rule of law. Thus, in an ideal sense, the 'public sphere' necessarily encourages both a diversity of opinion and practice as well as the conditions for dissent from majoritarian pressures.

Right from the outset, the public sphere in the Indian nation state has been a stillborn baby. It has been unable to prevent a high degree of information denial, advertisement-induced consumer slavery, mass surveillance, media-generated dumbing down and collective hysterical behaviour thriving on pathological violence.

If even after almost seventy years, our statistics throw up absurd figures like 34 per cent of the population living on less than US $1 a day or, in other words, some 400 million people living on less than ₹70 a day, the notion of the 'public sphere' becomes largely abstract. It, in fact, becomes a space from where the forces of Hindutva can mount an attack on the infructuous state. It becomes a site for both lumpen and elite vigilantism, for mystical revivalism, for majoritarian fascism and for militant Maoism.

The cultural commons and the discourse within it has been systematically usurped now by mainstream cinema with its cynical messages on the status quo or glorification of the violent hero or neurotic appeals to the divine. This has become the staple mass consumption.

Supplementing it is the contagion of mass

mysticism. Satsangs and bhajan mandalis have become the new polluters of the public mind, where literally millions of people are administered their daily dose on the virtues of conformism to the brutal, savage, caste-dominated society they live within.

Any resistance to this is dealt with systematically. The attempts over the past few months to hound NGOs, lawyers, media persons and fact-finding teams out of Chhattisgarh, for example, are dangerous portents and the official efforts to create a cordon sanitaire in the area so that no one may inform, comment or critique or even witness the large scale 'developmental' programmes destined for this Adivasi belt, is a possible preview to the large-scale violence to come.

XV

And the cascading violence has also turned unrepentant. A lad in Palanpur is lynched for eloping with a girl. In Bhagalpur, a petty thief is beaten up by a mob and then, in full view of TV cameras, tied to a police motorcycle and dragged through the streets till he falls unconscious.

Principals and professors of colleges are dragged

out, assaulted and killed. Fatwas are issued for cross-dressed religious leaders in Punjab or feminist writers like Taslima Nasreen. The Bhandarkar Oriental Research Institute in Pune ends up endorsing the violent censorship that wrecked its own research library. The offices of media institutions like *Dinakaran* in Madurai and *Outlook* in Mumbai are ransacked and torched for 'opinion polls' which disseminate results unpalatable to some parties. Caste panchayats across the country now increasingly determine how people should live or dress or love or marry.

Films like *Fire*, *Water*, *Parzania*, *Jo Bole So Nihaal*, *Rang de Basanti*, *Jashn-e-Azadi* are attacked; plays like *Ponga Pandit*, *The Vagina Monologues* are threatened, artists like M. F. Husain, Surendran Nair, Bhupen Khakhar, Arpita Singh, etc. are pilloried.

Of course, it must be mentioned that the blueprint for such virulent street violence was drawn up earlier, in 1984, during the all-India anti-Sikh pogroms in the wake of the assassination of Indira Gandhi. That is when the Indian state officially decided that it would henceforth speak through the mobs.

Since 1992, however, Hindutva brigades, proclaiming themselves custodians of social morality, have conducted several street operations. The domain of artistic expression, in fact, has come in for special attention. Art criticism in India now comes with a cutting edge.

Literally. Pens have been replaced by pen-knives. The new critics swing together in shoals of thirty, forty, hundred connoisseurs. They pay periodic visits to art galleries (like the one, some years ago, at Surat), where they display equal interest in the works of pioneers of contemporary Indian art like N. S. Bendre, radical pioneers like K. H. Ara and M. F. Husain and young modernists like Chittrovanu Mazumdar; stage plays (like Habib Tanvir's *Ponga Pandit* in many towns of Madhya Pradesh); or even libraries of rare manuscripts (like the Bhandarkar Oriental Research Institute, as I mentioned earlier).

Even as mainstream Indian media seems to collectively shut out serious arts coverage, comment or critique (rendering the individual 'critic' redundant), a new cabal of critics has taken to the streets. They fly diverse flags—the Vishwa Hindu Parishad, Bajrang Dal, Shiv Sena, Sambhaji Brigade, Sri Ram Sene. Yet their critical sensibilities are distinguished by suspicious similarities. They believe in instant judgement and in swift enforcement of aesthetic yardsticks (and stones). Scar, tar, mar is their preferred mode of critical practice.

The new Indian aesthetes (who seem to have no qualms emulating the deep cultural tutelage of the Taliban) do not place much value on what 'pleases' in art. They focus selectively on what 'offends'. And that's a pretty broad criterion to apply. For one can offend with anything.

Humour, irony, sarcasm, candour, irreverence, imagined insults to imagined cultural values or traditions, anything can instigate their critical faculties. In the blink of an eye they can pull out their idle kerosene cans and matchboxes and apply their well-practised pyromania on the offending object.

These 'cultural zappeurs' (organized street squads that zap you) are forever alert and active. They track individual artists. They ambush auditoria. They throttle theatre. They are cynical of serious cinema. They dread documentaries (*Muzaffarnagar Baaqi Hai* is their current target). '*Apologize, or else!*' becomes their magic mantra for regulating a compliant art.

The 'little man' that political psychologist Wilhelm Reich so beseeched us to beware of has now turned critic. We are squarely into the era of an aesthetic of erasures where it is not creativity that will evoke pleasure, but destruction. Here, destruction is the magical antiseptic in the hands of necrophilic agents, to be used on what seems 'offensive and impure' in order to maintain social hygiene.

Perhaps the day is not far off when a casual tourist to our cities will be able to identify the location of a handful of art galleries there by the quantum of police bandobast around it.

Poets, painters, playwrights, dancers, filmmakers often come up with views quite divergent from accepted beliefs or familiar and comfortable positions. Artists have claimed a space that has the potential to undermine, disturb, subvert the status quo. In fact, their art consists in their very ability, in Umberto Eco's phrase, to perennially 'carry out a new and subtle guerrilla warfare at the borders of meanings'.

But violent chastisement for having transgressed imagined boundaries of the permissible is now considered a legitimate activity by votaries of Hindutva. Way back, in 1993, senior ideologues of the Sangh Parivar like L. K. Advani, K. R. Malkani and others had attempted to publicly instruct M. F. Husain on how and what to paint. In 1996, VHP president Ashok Singhal had warned Husain to 'ceremonially burn' his 'offending' paintings of Saraswati to demonstrate his 'good intentions'. A far more belligerent Uma

Bharti had also recommended 'psychiatric treatment' for Husain. Of course, they eventually managed to hound him out of the country to die abroad.

Since those days in 1993, the art appreciation brigade of the Hindutva flank has not missed a trick in drumming up the bogey of uncontrolled art leading to social prurience, eroding of cultural values and, more significantly, simply being critical.

There is a well-articulated middle class conceit that the cut/slash/rip/dig formula of art appreciation is the dark hubris of a loony fringe of the Sangh Parivar. They would assure us that these are small and isolated incidents, whose perpetrators are mere lumpen madcaps, and should not be confused with the otherwise sane and cultured lot of the Parivar. Well, perhaps the news needs to be delivered to these worthies—the fringe has, in fact, usurped the field.

◆

We now come full circle to where we started. The journey from the initial attempts to construct a national culture, which was not sufficiently contested with respect to its Hindutva flavour, has progressively delivered us into the courtyard of cultural nationalism.

It should be clear by now that the ideology of cultural nationalism does not depend upon state power for its sustenance. On the contrary, its influence arises from its ability to manipulate power through displacement of parliamentary processes with wilful harangue, intimidation and systematic violence. Nationalism then is the trope that legitimizes its unrepentant aggression on every instrument of democracy. Nationalism will then also have to be the platform on which all such cynical battles are creatively resisted and unpacked.

ACKNOWLEDGEMENTS

The publishers would like to thank *Frontline* magazine for permission to use the essay 'Nationalism and its Contemporary Discontents in India' by A. G. Noorani. It first appeared as two essays in the magazine entitled 'Colonial Relic' (15 April 2016) and 'Nationalism vs Hindutva' (29 April 2016); these essays have been revised and edited by the author for publication in this book.

NOTES AND REFERENCES

FOREWORD

x   'Nationalism is not to be confused with patriotism...': George Orwell, 'Notes on Nationalism', 1945, http://orwell.ru/library/essays/nationalism/english/e_nat#fnt_1, accessed 30 May 2016.

xiii   'I do not believe there is any place...': Bombay Legislative Assembly Debates, Vol. 3, 4 April 1938, pp 1692-93.

REFLECTIONS ON NATIONALISM AND HISTORY

10   **influential book:** Benedict Anderson, *Imagined Communities: Reflections on the Origin and Spread of Nationalism*, 2010 (rev edn).

19   **This emerged as an ideology:** see Aimé Césaire, *Discourse on Colonialism*, 1950, trans., 1972; Léopold Senghor, *Nation et Voie Africaine du Socialisme*, 1961; and Léon Damas, *Poètes d'expression française*, 1946—the introduction to this anthology discusses Negritude.

NATIONALISM AND ITS CONTEMPORARY DISCONTENTS IN INDIA

62   'Take again Section 124A...': Parliamentary Debates, Volume XII, Part II, col 9621 (29 May 1951).

63   **If an apology be needed:** W. R. Donogh, *A Treatise on the Law of*

Sedition and Cognate Offences in British India, Penal and Preventive, 1911, https://archive.org/stream/onlawofsedition00dono/ onlawofsedition00dono_djvu.txt, accessed 30 May 2016.

64 **This law was substantially the same:** Ibid.

65 **'so as to make it efficient…':** Ibid.

68 **'Disaffection may be excited…':** Ibid.

69 **'even if there is nothing to show…':** *Queen Empress vs Bal Gangadhar Tilak,* ILR 22 Bom.112 (1897).

70 **'This is not the case…':** J. Ghosal (ed), *Celebrated Trials in India,* 1902, pp. 165-232.

71 **'It will be impossible to ignore the fact…':** A. G. Noorani, *Indian Political Trials 1775-1947,* 2005, p. 236.

72 **'reasonable anticipation…':** *Niharendu Dutt Majumdar vs The King Emperor,* 1942 Federal Court Reports 38.

72 **overruled him:** *King Emperor vs Sadashiv Narayan Bhalerao,* (1947), Indian Appeals 89.

72 **'The ordinary law of sedition…':** Ram Manohar Lohia, *The Struggle for Civil Liberties,* 1937, p. 42.

72 **The Draft Report of the Constituent Assembly's:** B. Shiva Rao (Ed.) *The Framing of India's Constitution,* Volume II, p. 139.

73 **'or undermines the authority…':** Ibid, p. 220.

73 **'The word "sedition"…':** *Constituent Assembly Debates,* Volume VIII, p. 731.

75 **deliberate, considered decision:** B. Shiva Rao, *The Framing of India's Constitution,* Vol. IV, p. 755.

76 **'It is also worthy of note…':** *Romesh Thapar vs State of Madras,* AIR 1950 SC 124 at 128.

76 **Master Tara Singh's case:** AIR 1952 Punjab 27.

77 **'The section has become inappropriate…':** Ibid, p. 403.

78 **'the Penal Code contained…':** James Fitzjames Stephen, *A History of the Criminal Law of England,* Vol III, p. 308.

79   **A full bench of three judges:** *Ram Nandan vs State.*

80   **'Today the dogs of the C. I. D…':** *Kedar Nath Singh vs State of Bihar:* AIR 1962 SC 955; (1963) 1 SCJ 18

81   **'This species of offence…':** Ibid.

84   ***Balwant Singh & ANR. vs State of Punjab:*** (1995) 3 SCC 214.

84   ***Bilal Ahmed Kaloo vs State of Andhra Pradesh:*** AIR 1997 SCC 431.

84   **'Section 124-A deals with…':** *Nazir Khan vs State of Delhi,* (2003) 8 SCC 461.

86   **the constitutional guarantees of free speech:** *Brandenburg vs Ohio* 395 US 444 (1969).

86   **the mere abstract teaching:** *Noto v United States,* 367 US 290, 297-298, (1961).

87   **'In a free democratic society…':** *Hector vs Attorney-General of Antigua,* 2AC 312 (1990).

89   **in defence of Thomas Paine…:** Thomas Paine was tried for seditious libel on 18 December 1792, in response to his publication of the second part of the *Rights of Man,* which advocated the right of the people to overthrow their government; Edward Walford, *The Rights of Man: Speeches of Thomas Lord Erskine,* Volumes 1 and 2, 1870.

89   **'the offence of seditious libel…':** Lord Alfred Denning, *Landmarks in the Law,* 1984, p. 295.

89   **'is frighteningly broad…':** Geoffrey Robertson, and Andrew Nicol, *Media Law: The Rights of Journalists and Broadcasters,* 1984.

90   **'Sedition and seditious and defamatory libel…':** Clare Feikert-Ahalt, Sedition in England: The Abolition of a Law From a Bygone Era, 2 Oct 2012, http://blogs.loc.gov/law/2012/10/sedition-in-england-the-abolition-of-a-law-from-a-bygone-era/, accessed 30 May 2016.

91   **There is no greater nonsense:** Hansard, HC, *vol 188 cols 2075-*

189 (1 December 1925).

92 *Gitlow vs New York:* 268 US 652 (1925).

93 'It is said that this manifesto...': Susan-Mary Grant, *Oliver Wendell Holmes, Jr.: Civil War Soldier, Supreme Court Justice,* 2016, p. 155.

94 If the nation cares for its values: See Donald Alexander Downs, *Restoring Free Speech and Liberty on Campus,* 2005.

95 Every individual and body or persons: Education (No. 2) Act, 1986, The National Archives, http://www.legislation.gov. uk/ukpga/1986/61/section/43, accessed 30 May 2016.

95 'anyone who refused to say...': 'RSS Says Owaisi 'Anti-national, BJP's Shah Looks to Other Factors', *The New Indian Express,* 17 March 2016.

95–96 'not tolerate criticism of the country', 'anti-national activity...': 'Anti-national activity can't be justified on the plea of freedom of expression: Amit Shah,' *DNA,* 19 March 2016.

96 Every stone here has a story: V. D. Savarkar, *Hindutva: Who is a Hindu,* https://archive.org/stream/hindutva-vinayak-damodar-savarkar-pdf/hindutva-vd-savarkar_djvu.txt, accessed 30 May 2016.

98 'I offer this work to the public...': Shamsul Islam, *Golwalkar's We or Our Nationhood Defined : A Critique,* 2006, p. 5.

98 'virtual anthem for the contemporary Hindutva movement': Chetan Bhatt, *Hindu Nationalism: Origins, Ideologies and Modern Myths,* 2001, p. 27.

98 'Hinduized nationalist slogan': Ibid, p. 22.

99 'Of considerable significance...': Ibid, p. 187.

100 'Durga, the goddess and the mother...': B. R. Purohit, *Hindu Revivalism and Indian Nationalism,* 1990, p. 79.

101 'Bankim...gave the project...': Yogesh Vajpeyi, *Indian Express,* 30 June 1998.

102 The two nationalisms: Purohit, *Hindu Revivalism.*

FROM NATIONAL CULTURE TO CULTURAL NATIONALISM

108 'The nation is the greatest evil': Rabindranath Tagore, *Nationalism*, 1917.

109 I'm an Indian: personal conversation with the author.

110 Albert Camus used the metaphor: See the novel *The Plague* (1947), trans. Robin Buss (2001).

114 Bal Gangadhar Tilak in his essay: 'The Arctic Home in the Vedas', https://ia802706.us.archive.org/5/items/ TheArcticHomeInTheVedas/TilakLokamanya-TheArcticHomeI nTheVedas1903470P..pdf, accessed 2 Jun 2016.

114 'Indian Civilization 7000 BCE': Luckily this embarrassing and infuriating installation got painted over soon after the UPA wrested power in 2002.

118 'nationalism absorbs traditions superficially...': see Mohinder Singh's essay in *Critical Studies in Politics: Explaining Sites, Selves, Power*, ed. Nivedita Menon et al, 2014.

119 war against 'outsiders': Sudipta Kaviraj, *The Unhappy Consciousness: Bankim Chandra Chattopadhyay and the Formation of Nationalist Discourse in India*, 1995.

122 'A national culture under colonial...': Frantz Fanon, *The Wretched of the Earth*, trans. Richard Philcox, 2004. Originally published in French in 1961.

135 'if [writers] are unable to write...': 'Let (writers) stop writing, then we will see: Culture Minister Mahesh Sharma', *Indian Express*, 13 Oct 2015.

135 'The atmosphere has become hateful...': Ibid.

136 'What is happening in India pains me...': Mir Ehsan, 'J&K writer Ghulam Nabi Khayal, Kannada writer Srinath D. N. return Sahitya Akademi award', *Indian Express*, 12 Oct 2015.

NOTES ON THE CONTRIBUTORS

Romila Thapar is Emeritus Professor of History at the Jawaharlal Nehru University, New Delhi. She has been General President of the Indian History Congress. She is a Fellow of the British Academy and holds an Hon D.Litt each from Calcutta University, Oxford University and the University of Chicago. She is an Honorary Fellow of Lady Margaret Hall, Oxford, and SOAS, London. In 2008, Professor Thapar was awarded the prestigious Kluge Prize of the US Library of Congress, which honours lifetime achievement in studies such as History that are not covered by the Nobel Prize.

A. G. Noorani is an Indian lawyer, historian and author. He has practised as an advocate in the Supreme Court of India and in the Bombay High Court. His columns have appeared in the *Hindustan Times*, *The Hindu*, *Frontline*, *Economic and Political Weekly* and *Dainik Bhaskar*. He is the author of a number of books, among them *The Kashmir Question*, *The Trial of Bhagat Singh*, *Constitutional Questions in India* and *The RSS and the BJP: A Division of Labour*. He is also the biographer of Badruddin Tyabji and Dr Zakir Hussain.

Sadanand Menon explores the charged space linking politics and culture through his work in media, pedagogy and the arts. He is Adjunct Faculty, Asian College of Journalism, Chennai and at IIT,

Madras. He has been an arts editor, columnist and photographer. He was a long-time collaborator of the late dancer/choreographer Chandralekha. He is also a leading stage lights designer. He has been on the Advisory Committees of the National Museum, National Gallery of Modern Art, Lalit Kala Akademi, National School of Drama and the Indian Institute of Advanced Study, Shimla. He is currently managing trustee of the Arts Foundation, SPACES, Chennai.

INDEX